THE ART OF THE POSSIBLE

THE ART OF THE
POSSIBLE

A HANDBOOK FOR POLITICAL ACTIVISM

AMANDA SUSSMAN

McClelland & Stewart

Library and Archives Canada Cataloguing in Publication

Sussman, Amanda
    The art of the possible : a handbook for social activists / Amanda Sussman.

ISBN 978-0-7710-8340-2

    1. Political participation – Canada. 2. Politics, Practical – Canada. 3. Canada – Social policy – Citizen participation. 4. Political planning – Canada – Citizen participation. I. Title.

JL186.5.S98 2007   324.0971   C2007-901439-9

We acknowledge the financial support of the Government of Canada through the Book Publishing Industry Development Program and that of the Government of Ontario through the Ontario Media Development Corporation's Ontario Book Initiative. We further acknowledge the support of the Canada Council for the Arts and the Ontario Arts Council for our publishing program.

Typeset in Electra by M&S, Toronto
Printed and bound in Canada

ANCIENT FOREST
FRIENDLY

McClelland & Stewart Ltd.
75 Sherbourne Street
Toronto, Ontario
M5A 2P9
www.mcclelland.com

1 2 3 4 5   11 10 09 08 07

For Lorna Sussman

CONTENTS

THE IDENTITY MORE THAN THE CAUSE

For as long as I can remember, I have had a vague desire to change the world. Like many Canadians, I feel relatively lucky with where I am in life, yet I feel a little nagging guilt that I should be doing more to make things better. That feeling was especially strong when I was fresh out of university. I had no idea what my cause was or what I was supposed to do about it, but still I couldn't shake the notion that I should try to do *something*.

In 1993 the headlines were screaming that sinister logging companies in British Columbia were moments away from tearing down old-growth forests like Clayoquot Sound. How could they do this? If there's one thing that makes Canada unique, it's our wilderness, and if we lose that what do we have?

I was living in Toronto and I envisioned Vancouver as Canada's version of Berkeley, California, in 1969: campfires on the beach, peace drums in the parks, and a community of social activists that could tell me what I could do to help. I wanted to live Mahatma Gandhi's phrase "be the change you want to see." That summer, I headed west. I put myself up at a beach house with six other people, became a vegetarian, wore peasant skirts, and joined up with Greenpeace. Gone was meat! Gone was furniture! Gone was footwear! (For some reason – I don't remember why – we also decided to forgo shoes.)

As the summer wore on, however, I began to notice that things weren't getting done – on any front. Clayoquot Sound was still set for demolition. Toxic waste continued to pollute the rivers and lakes. The only things that seemed to be getting accomplished were keeping the neighbourhood pot dealer wealthy and infuriating grocers with demands for more stringent background checks on brands that may have affiliations with oil companies.

I was involved in local fundraising and was generally frustrated by the lack of financial support I got from canvassing wealthy neighbourhoods to save Clayoquot Sound. I felt helpless. How was I going to change the world like this? Indeed, could I make any change at all? My stomach hurt, my feet were sore, and I was living in a dive. Is this what activism is really about? I knew that Greenpeace was achieving great things globally, but what difference was I making, between rolling joints and eating sunflower seeds?

Soon enough, a breakthrough came. One morning while going door-to-door, a family of loggers – loggers! – pledged my largest donation ever. They explained that they too were concerned about clear-cutting. They gave me details about alternative methods of logging that they wanted their union to support. We started an eye-opening discussion about the various political, labour, and environmental pressures involved. Suddenly I felt ridiculous. Here were the people who really knew what was going on and how to fix it. What did I know about selective forestry? It occurred to me that if I really wanted to make a difference, I might just have to do some homework.

That afternoon I curled up under a tree with a big bowl of juicy cherries and thought over my exciting discussion with the logging family. A co-worker from Greenpeace spotted me and made her way over to where I was sitting. I had looked up to her all summer. With her Indonesian pants, nose ring, and blond dreadlocks, she dared to go much farther than me on every enviro-fashion front. I started to tell her about the logger's labour situation and selective forestry. I looked up to see my colleague staring at my bowl of cherries with a horrified expression on her face: "Are those not organic?"

Were they? My god, here I was upbeat about the possibilities for change, and once again, I was part of the problem.

But . . . wait, who cared? Did it really matter? For the first time I started to see my group of activists through the eyes of the grocer across the street. Suddenly my righteousness had become self-righteousness. I knew that I loved the identity the environmental movement bestowed on me. But did I love the identity more than the cause? Would worrying about whether I was eating organic cherries actually make the world a better place? To be sure, buying organic can change the world if we garner enough support to shift global demand. In the meantime, though, how could I actually get something done?

Shortly after, I put on my shoes and went for a steak.

My change of direction led to a series of experiences that form the basis of this book. Instead of searching for an identity as a revolutionary, I wanted to understand how things really worked. My journey took me from Amnesty International and Human Rights Watch to the Department of Foreign Affairs and the UN. From Paul Wolfowitz and Bill Graham to Sergio de Mello and Kofi Annan, I've studied, worked for, and had access to people who made decisions that affect thousands of lives in very real ways.

This book is about the art of the possible. It is a compilation of what I've learned about how decisions get made. It offers a practical guide for citizens who want to get involved beyond elections. Change does happen, but it happens in small steps. My focus is on incremental reform, which is both the triumph and frustration of democracy.

For instance, there were no gay rights or feminist "revolutions" that shook the foundations of our institutions and transformed society overnight. Rather, change happened through the difficult process of democratic advocacy. From the standpoint of social justice, our big gains have all come from measured reform within the system. Change occurred through the slow process of democratic participation: people making arguments, building coalitions, lobbying for legislative change, and, when necessary, refusing to abide by laws they view as unjust.[1] In the blink of history, it may have seemed like a revolution, but in reality, it happened at an incremental pace.

The first question that many in government would ask of advocates is "Well, who elected you?" As a citizen or a citizen working in a group, you represent a particular interest, whereas the government's job is to represent all our interests. In our model of responsible government, it is the role of members of Parliament (M.P./M.P.P.) to act as the legitimate check on government authority.[2] Every Canadian is directly represented in the House of Commons by an elected M.P., so why should the government listen directly to you?

Parliament acts as the ultimate check and balance against executive power, but there are a multitude of decisions made every day that never go to Parliament for deliberation. In the system we've got, parliament

---

[1] Joseph Heath and Andrew Potter, *The Rebel Sell: Why Culture Can't Be Jammed* (Harper Collins, 2004) p. 9.

[2] "Responsible government" means that the prime minister, the cabinet ministers, and the departments that support them are accountable to Parliament. For more on the Canadian system of parliamentary democracy see C.E.S. Franks, *The Parliament of Canada* (University of Toronto Press, 1987).

does not play a major role in developing policy. Moreover, while Cabinet provides the critical forum for politicians to question policies proposed by bureaucracies, it does not have the time or capacity to evaluate more than the broad strokes of a major policy decision. At a minimum, a strong, informed network of citizen's groups is necessary to follow the details of government policy carefully and keep check on the host of delegated decisions that are made every day.

My intent is not to contribute to the body of literature on democratic reform. Those much more qualified than I are currently in the midst of discussions on the merits of strengthening the role of the M.P. in scrutinizing policy. Proposals for reform include such things as increasing the time, the money, and the capacity M.P.s have to effectively participate in policy-making. Rather, I take it as given that policy is now so vast and so complex there is a need to strengthen both the role of citizens and of M.P.s in order to get the best possible information to decision-makers and hold them accountable for their decisions. My goal is simply to help make interactions between citizens and their government more effective so that we can produce the best policy we can.

During my time as human rights adviser to two federal cabinet ministers, I was offered a bird's-eye view of how government works, and why certain people are more successful than others in having a tangible impact on policy. In this book, I have also included the views of dozens of officials, activists, members of Parliament, senior political advisers, former ministers, and well-known politicians. My aim is to offer the best collective advice to those on the outside who seek to challenge the government from within.

This book doesn't argue for a particular cause. The cause is up to you. That being said, the examples will draw on my experiences working on issues of human rights. For all causes, however, I do argue that to be effective, advocates need to start by considering some fundamental questions about themselves and how they want to work.

ARE YOU A RADICAL OR ARE YOU A REFORMER?

The first questions an activist needs to ask are these: Are you happy striving for an ideal, even if you may never reach it? Do you need to see immediate progress, even if it's small, to keep you going? Do you want to remain on the outside of government fighting for your ideal or are you willing to negotiate from within?

Radicalism, in the sense of getting to the root of a matter and pushing for fundamental change, is important.[3] Often, if you want to achieve anything, you have to push for everything. If the harshest critics of the World Bank and the International Monetary

---

[3] This is to be distinguished from extremism – a political ideology favouring uncompromising adherence to a particular body of doctrines or beliefs. Here the term "radical" refers to favouring drastic political, economic, or social change from accepted or traditional forms. It is also to be completely dissociated from the use of violence, which has no place in a functioning democracy such as ours.

Fund (IMF) were not demanding the institutions' very demise, there would be little incentive for decision-makers to do more than tinker with the status quo.

But where there is a radical on one side, there is usually a radical on the other. The reason for democracy is essentially to keep these radicals in check.

To do this, we allow for opposing points of view and elect our leaders to find a compromise with which we can all live. For a decision to be both legitimate and sustainable, it must have some degree of buy-in on all sides. For good leaders, compromise doesn't have to mean finding the lowest common denominator. Rather, they take the best ideas, test them against their critics, and allow for adjustments where it makes sense.

This book does not ignore the radical approach. Protests, boycotts, and alternative summits send out the important message that there *is* a problem, and that it needs to be solved. Leaders have to take notice and consider the need for change. But if you're interested in a change of a specific policy, this book argues that the greatest of changes occur from within. Reform does not mean compromising your basic values.[4] Rather than rejecting government, it demonstrates how working through government is the most direct route to social progress. It means understanding where your bottom lines are and where you have room to manoeuvre.

---

[4] By "reform" I mean to improve by alteration, correction of error, or removal of defects; to put into a better form or condition.

To illustrate this point, let's take a look at the G8 summits, the most prominent targets for social activists today. At Gleneagles and Heiligendamm, the anti-globalization movement sent a message that no global-ization was good globalization. Images of alternative kids, dressed in alternative clothes, garnered public attention with demands to shut the G8 meetings down.

One can understand where they are coming from. According to many activists, governments have little power in the face of rising corporate influence. In many parts of the world, it is multinational corpo-rations that are providing for basic human needs like clean water, sanitation, and access to health care. In the developed world, major social change is taking place outside the political world, with government playing a peripheral or even obstructive role. Progress on gay rights is being won through the courts. Fair trade is being promoted by progressive companies rather than by parliaments or government depart-ments.[5] As a result, rather than spend time working through government institutions, many radicals focus their energies on consumer boycotts, corporate aware-ness campaigns, and shareholder politics.

After the G8 summits,[6] many were frustrated that no matter how big the protests got or how widespread the message, there seemed to be few results. From the perspective of those inside these meetings, the radical

---

[5] Jebediah Purdy, "After Apathy," *The American Prospect*, Vol. 11, No. 2 (Dec. 6, 1999).

[6] G8 countries include Canada, the United States, England, France, Russia, Germany, Italy, and Japan.

approach to advocacy backfired. Leaders and officials were left with the impression that these were fringe elements of society wanting the impossible: rolling back globalization, ceasing all international trade, dismantling the World Bank, the International Monetary Fund, and the World Trade Organization, and starting from scratch.

That is not to say that the protests didn't achieve anything. Widespread public awareness and involvement in an issue build a powerful constituency of support to which democratic politicians ultimately have to respond.

But to have an impact on the actual decisions and policies announced by governments at the G8, you have to start much earlier than the main event. It requires working from the bottom up and the top down of government to convince internal and external advocates of the merits of your position, address the concerns of those who disagree, and offer plausible options that take into account real government constraints.

More often than not, a "win" will not go far enough, fast enough. Every step taken will open up a whole array of new miles that need to be trod. But with many government decisions, even an incremental step can affect hundreds of lives. What seems like a small decision can actually have a huge impact.

WE NEED YOU MORE THAN EVER

Post-September 11, the reformist route is even harder. Within national governments security trumps all.

The extreme and rare cases – the shoe bomber aboard a commercial airliner about to detonate – are now the starting point for many government decisions. Although extreme cases make bad law, it is these cases that have shaped recent legislation and dominated policy discussions.

We rely on government departments to use their resources and experience to develop expert, non-partisan advice for our politicians to consider. But it can be dangerous when policy is left to departments alone. For a politician, once officials present an issue as "Minister, this is a matter of national security," he or she has no choice but to take a better-safe-than-sorry approach. In the current context, whatever the political party, politicians and bureaucrats alike feel it would be irresponsible not to do so. The cost of underestimating a potential terrorist threat will always outweigh the cost of overestimating one.

For this reason there is an urgent need for more outside individuals and organizations to get in there and tackle the difficult security questions head on. Although it can be uncomfortable, advocates need to consider the extreme cases that force government to make hard decisions they would rather avoid. Beyond security, the only way to be sure that other points of view are presented is to do more than just vote.

When the election is over, the need for informed citizen participation does not diminish. By building organizations and coalitions, citizens have an important role to play in helping shape government policy.

Policy is not a distant invention created by faceless officials behind closed doors. Policy is what shapes the society you live in, the environment around you, and the opportunities available to help you achieve your potential. With the political pendulum swinging even farther toward hard-line positions, there is a need for citizens directly affected by policy to help develop alternative solutions that are feasible from the government's point of view. And these alternatives must be presented at the right time – before departments present ministers with impossible choices framed in a way they cannot refuse.

WHY GET INVOLVED?

What difference can one person make? If I'm not a renowned millionaire, famous actor, or rock star, what do I really have to offer?

The notion that the government is open only to a few is a myth. In fact, our political system is incredibly accessible. What is threatening our democracy is a dangerous apathy and misguided belief that people can participate only through elections. Many people feel that they cannot have an impact on the specific decisions that affect their lives. They see government as so complex and distant that there is really no point in trying to make a difference. But democracy is not only for the well-funded, entrenched, or few. It is a remarkable political system that includes all of us. This book is a tool to make your participation count. It will help you understand how you can change the world in clear, effective, measurable ways.

No matter how old you are or where you are in life, you can still have an impact on the decisions that shape the world around you. Maybe you are young, just out of high school, or in university, and don't want to study theories of political change – you want to know how to make an actual difference. You could be motivated by a single issue you read about that affects your life or those you care about. You know that if you don't express your views, those with the opposite opinion will express theirs and you want all sides of the issue to be included in the public debate. Rather than observe from the sidelines, you want to be part of the social and political movements that change history and influence the decisions that affect your life.

Or maybe you are mid-career and feeling a bit bored or disillusioned with the career path you chose. Ten years on, you have achieved a certain degree of success in your work but feel you would like to devote more time and energy to a meaningful cause. You may have observed a problem in your community or environment and you want to find a way to effectively draw the government's attention to it.

Alternatively, your motivation may be the work you do – one issue may be having a profound impact on your profession, your organization, or those whom it serves. The government may have made a decision that has a negative effect on you personally or your institution's ability to achieve its mission or goals. You feel you have the experience and expertise required to help shape better public policy decisions for those in your field.

Perhaps you are recently retired and finally have the time and money to devote to doing what you want to do. The only problem is that you are not sure how to begin. You know the government needs fresh solutions and you have a lifetime of experience that may suggest a better way to get things done.

These are all good reasons to get involved, and it's important to remember that the more you participate, the more democratic our country will be.

HOW IT CAN BE DONE

Elected politicians have the power to make decisions, but the bureaucracy has the power to make them happen. For advocacy to work, policy alternatives must get a critical mass of people on side at every stage of decision-making. Being a successful advocate does not mean having your view adopted exactly as you proposed it. Rather, success means that your information is on the right table, before the right people, at the right time.

This book will help you do just that. The following offers a step-by-step guide to creating a successful strategy that leads to real change.

STEP 1: Research

The first step to developing your advocacy plan is to make sure that you have done the basic research so that your position on an issue is both relevant and credible. In general you will want to scan the following sources in order to be aware of what the government is currently doing and how it is framing its priorities.

- Recent newspaper clippings, from a variety of sources
- Government Web sites related to your issue
- Recent ministerial speeches
- The Speech from the Throne
- Any parliamentary reports on your topic
- The Web sites of the major advocacy organizations concerned with your issue

Covering this preliminary step will help to build your credibility by demonstrating that you are well-briefed on the issue before you begin.

If you have the time and resources, it is always a good idea to probe more deeply into your research. What was done under previous governments? Was your idea tried in the past? Is there an international precedent? The more you know about the political history of a proposed policy, the better prepared you will be to deal with any upcoming obstacles to seeing your proposal become a reality.

STEP 2: Connect with Others

While individuals can and do make a difference, working with others is the best way to bolster your case and strengthen the impact of your actions. Give some thought to whom you want to work with and why. It is important that you are comfortable with the values, style, and methods of those around you. Research the existing opportunities provided by the established organizations and/or make contact with smaller groups coming together around a specific cause.

STEP 3: Identify Your Resources

How much time, money, or effort are you willing to put into your campaign? Be realistic about your level of commitment so you can strategically plan how to spend those resources and make sure you can follow through.

Make a decision on the intensity of the advocacy campaign to be pursued. Campaigns can be categorized as low, medium, or high; each requires a different level of commitment.

STEP 4: Develop a Clear Objective

Your recommendations to government should be specific, measurable, achievable, realistic, and time-bound (SMART). Once you have drafted your recommendations to government, ask yourself the following questions: What is the specific "ask"? What are the reasons for your request? Who is the recommendation directed at? How can it be done?

To help answer these questions, be clear about what type of change you are advocating:

- Legislative change – requires an amendment to an existing law or a proposal for a new law.
- Regulatory change – requires a change to a government regulation, which does not go through Parliament.
- Political policy change – requires a decision at the cabinet or ministerial level to change a government policy.
- Departmental policy change – requires a change

in the guidelines given to officials who make decisions based on delegated authority.

Once you have developed a clear objective, evaluate your expectations for what you view as success. If you have asked someone for something that is within their power to do, you have a much better chance of seeing concrete results. If your objective is specific, realistic, and measurable, you should be able to identify points of progress along the way. This will help you maintain your motivation and encourage the efforts of others.

STEP 5: Secure Internal Support

Before you move forward, make sure there is consensus within your group on the specific objective to be pursued. It is important that all internal disagreements remain internal. As soon as divisions are exposed between you and your allies, the message to politicians is "You're damned if you do and you're damned if you don't."

Once the objective is settled, choose an agreed-upon representative to communicate a united position to outsiders. Make sure that the person has a clear mandate to speak on behalf of the entire group. At the same time, that person should also have some leeway to negotiate specific wording or adjust a position to some degree so they can actively participate in policy discussions with decision-makers responsible for reflecting more than one point of view.

STEP 6: Develop Key Messages

How you ask a question largely determines its answer. In politics, like any other field, the language you use to describe your issue is critically important. Citizens can play a major role in framing the debate on an issue they care about. Building on the work you have done to identify your specific advocacy objectives, develop key messages that are tailored to a number of different audiences. While your fundamental objectives and goals should not change, be sure that you can communicate them effectively to people with different levels of knowledge and experience of your issue. Be prepared with short concise statements to communicate your cause to political leaders, government officials, the media, and the general public. While messages to the media, government officials, and politicians may be framed differently, make sure that you are strictly consistent in the overall content of your message.

STEP 7: Identify Allies and Opponents

Make a list of organizations currently working on your issue and identify where there may be opportunities for partnership. Whether you decide to join forces or not, be clear about where you are aligned with other organizations and where there are differences. Also identify unlikely allies. Police associations, church groups, or business leaders may all have a reason for supporting your cause. Third-party endorsements can add a lot of strength to your case.

The more diversified your coalition, the more powerful your arguments become.

During this stage it is also critical to research where the opposition is coming from. To strengthen your argument and guard it against its most likely critics, develop an understanding of and respect for those who disagree with your way of thinking. Spend some time anticipating where the issue may get stuck. Some of the most common reasons that governments are constrained from taking action are problems with jurisdiction, timing, and internal or external opposition. Looking at your issue from different perspectives will help you be prepared to respond to criticism in advance.

STEP 8: Create a Reasonable Timeline

Most importantly, create an advocacy timeline that revolves around dates that are significant for your particular issue. Plot on it any relevant international events that you may be aware of, from UN (United Nations) assemblies and G8 summits to regular meetings of organizations such as NATO (North Atlantic Treaty Organization), OAS (Organization of American States), APEC (Asia-Pacific Economic Cooperation), or the WTO (World Trade Organization). Also incorporate the major domestic events that occupy the government's attention throughout the year. These include the budget, the Speech from the Throne, significant parliamentary hearings, or days designated to commemorate special events.

Creating a detailed timeline is essential to any good strategy. It will reveal the political context in which all your efforts are taking place. Knowing the context will save you time and money by helping you to identify when to make your interventions so they have the best chance of having an effect.

It's also important to select a timeline that works for you. Will you follow and act on the issue for one year? Six months? Three years? It's always a good idea to tailor your expectations to the time you can put in. Experienced activists know that major campaigns (like the Jubilee Debt Campaign, which was an international effort to stop developed countries from collecting debt from the world's most impoverished nations) need at least three to five years. On the other hand, local issues may need only as long as between now and the next vote at city council. Whatever your cause, the time frame you select should give you enough time to research properly, make contact with others working on the issue, and plan a feasible number of activities given your available resources.

STEP 9: Choose Your Tactics and Plan Your Advocacy Activities

Whether you choose to start a letter-writing campaign, meet with officials, run a pilot project, hold a press conference, or organize a demonstration, the timeline you have outlined should help to indicate which activities will be most effective given the political context in which they will take place. It will also help you decide when to meet or call certain officials and when to schedule meetings with an M.P. or a minister. If you are sensitive to the internal priorities of government, it's possible to approach the right people when they are most likely to be most receptive to your request.

STEP 10: Implement Your Plan but Be Flexible

Follow through with your plan! Organize your resources so that you place the emphasis on the activities that are likely to have the most impact. Throughout your designated period, however, be sure to monitor the timing of your advocacy activities to see that they continue to make the best use of your resources. Above all, allow for flexibility and be prepared to change tactics if necessary. If new information hints that an upcoming meeting isn't likely to be all that useful, don't hesitate to back down and wait for a better time. Officials would prefer to reschedule rather than go ahead with a meeting when they have no power to respond to concerns. Similarly, if in your meetings with government officials you learn more about where internal opposition is coming from, adjust your activities and messaging as needed.

When necessary, hold periodic meetings within your group or organization to update your strategy continuously. It is important to evaluate your work to make sure that each effort is directly useful to achieving your overall goal. If you or others identify obstacles that cannot be overcome in the near future, work on other aspects of the issue until they can be resolved.

A final evaluation at the end of your time frame will help you answer the question of whether you achieved what you set out to do.

DON'T GET DISCOURAGED!

There's no feeling like the feeling of success. I remember a small insert I made to a speech that was drafted by the Department of Foreign Affairs for the minister to make at the United Nations. This was during the buildup to the current war in Iraq. The speech was talking about the importance of "fighting for freedom." I added an arrow and scribbled in the margins, "We need to be clear on what we mean by 'freedom.' In today's world, the fight for freedom too often ignores freedom of expression, freedom of association, and freedom from arbitrary detention." A few days later, Colin Powell gave his now infamous presentation to the Security Council, where he tried to convince the rest of the world that the case for war in Iraq was justified. I saw that Canada was there on record, with this ominous warning, before all the countries of the world. Of course, Canada's decision not to go to war in Iraq was a lot more complex than one speech, but for me, successfully recommending one statement that pointed us in the right direction was enough to keep me going for years to come.

Once you experience that first small victory, it's easy to become hooked on political activism for life. Have no illusions. Advocacy is by no means easy. There are times when you'll want to tear your hair out. We will always have a lot to learn as we go. But whoever you are and wherever you're placed, it is possible to have an impact on the decisions that affect your life. Whether you are just one person with a few hours per week to devote to your cause or a large organization with a whole array of resources at your disposal, I hope this book will stop you from thinking about whether or not do it, and start you thinking about how it can be done.

CHAPTER ONE

WHERE DO YOU START?

Taking the First Step

How do you get over that initial feeling of inertia and start to take action? One way is to start local, on an issue you live with every day, and build your confidence and experience from there. The story of Elinor Caplan is a great example. As a mother of four, Elinor noticed that the kids in her neighbourhood had to navigate a dangerous, unmarked crossing on their way to school. She began her career by pushing for a crosswalk at that perilous intersection. After gathering community support and making the case to municipal officials, she felt the satisfaction of seeing the installation of a new crosswalk. The crosswalk success gave her the confidence to run for municipal council, then provincially in Ontario as an M.P.P., (after which she was made minister of Health) and finally federally as an M.P., being rewarded with the role of minister of

Citizenship and Immigration and then minister of National Revenue. Whether it is student politics, community decisions, or a fight within any institution, a good place to start is in your own backyard.

BUT WHAT CAN YOU DO?

One of the most powerful things citizens can do is *reframe public policy questions from an alternative perspective*. To "frame" an issue means choosing the language to define a political debate and fitting individual issues into a publicly understandable story.

As a citizen or organization working outside of government, you can play a part in reframing the debate on the issues you care about. How you pose a question largely determines its answer. Whether the question refers to security, the environment, trade, health care, or foreign policy, the language you use directly affects the options presented for consideration and the ultimate policy decisions taken by the government.[1]

Of course, activism is not just about language. It's about ideas. There have to be substantial ideas based on sound research and thorough analysis before language becomes your main concern. Although government departments are the central locale for developing and evaluating policy options for the government to consider, citizens can also help develop the solutions to the problems that affect them directly. Regardless of your political persuasion, it is important to continually challenge established ideas and frames

---

[1] See Chapter 8 for a more detailed discussion on reframing issues.

so that decision-makers have real options from which to choose.

But if you have only limited time and resources, how can activism possibly be worthwhile? Even if you have one hour per week to put in, that one hour per week can lead to a rich sense of satisfaction. A good meeting with the right official or an event that sparks public interest at the right time can make an invaluable contribution.

Naturally, overhauling government policy on broader and far-reaching issues will require more time. However, as long as your definition of success correlates to what you are able to devote to an issue, you will find that participating and effecting change will add to your life, to your sense of self-fulfilment, and, most importantly, to the broader community in which you live.

Clearly, working alone is not going to be most effective. Behind even the most charismatic activist is a rich network of community organizations supporting their efforts to achieve social change. Individuals may spearhead an idea, but it takes steady community support and participation for a project to go from the idea stage to fruition.

Government is not the monolithic, impenetrable fortress it appears to be. Like most large organizations or companies, it is made up of individuals, each playing a part in shaping the overall actions and decisions their institution takes. In Canada, organizing even on a small scale can have a big impact. If you follow one particular issue, you will soon find that after

a short while, you will be familiar with the key organizations and individuals that have been active on the
topic for years. The amazing thing from a policy perspective is that it is possible to gather a somewhat comprehensive picture of who the key activists are from
different sides of the issue and where they are coming
from. Although this will certainly not cover everyone
in the country who has an opinion on the topic, you
can get a good grasp of the landscape and be well
informed on the various points of view.

The size of this country also gives us an opportunity to demand that our politicians truly be representative. It never ceased to amaze me that in Canada, if
you are well prepared and understand how the government works, you can actually sit down with a minister and tell them what you think. Elected officials,
whether they are a backbench M.P., a member of the
Opposition, or a minister, will listen when confronted
by even a small group of well-informed constituents.
They know they have to if they are to continue to represent that constituency to government.

How does one individual take that first step? For
those just beginning, here is a list of six practical steps
on how to start. Of course, in the real world working
on an issue is more fluid than linear but the objective
here is to offer a reference point when you're not sure
what to do next.

STEP 1: Select Your Topic Carefully
If you are looking for a worthwhile way to spend your
time but don't know what that means for you, start by

examining your personal interests and values. While the topic you choose will likely have broader community and social implications, it is important that you choose something that has meaning in your life.

With regard to interests – are there particular issues that consistently irk you? Whether you read about it in the paper or confront it in your daily life, is there a specific topic you have come to know a lot about simply because you are interested in it? Is there a certain organization you admire? Why? Examining your interests will help make sure you choose a topic that will sustain your attention. To have an impact and see a result for your efforts, you want to choose an issue that will continue to hold your interest over a defined period of time.

With regard to values – are there particular social principles that are especially relevant to you? Universal health care, global poverty, support for the arts, public education, children's rights, women's rights, and environmental responsibility are all examples of areas that may coincide with your personal values. Is there an area that you have experience with? Is there one that you feel strongly enough about to focus on and devote some time and energy to? Choosing a topic that resonates with you personally will help make your efforts less of a burden and more of a release. Spending your time addressing the problems that bother you deeply rather than lamenting about them can give you a real sense of personal satisfaction, regardless of the outcome. Instead of watching the issue unfold and feeling helpless in the process, you can join with others and gain a sense of control by taking concrete steps to address the problem and discover the power you have to affect the solution.

Then make a conscious decision as to whether to leave your topic fairly open and general or whether to narrow it down to something very specific. General topics may be thematic, but not too broad. If you are interested in the "environment," for example, break it down into its various components. Which aspects of the environment are you interested in? Clean water? Power generation? Air pollution? Energy efficiency?

Choosing a general thematic topic gives you the advantage of being more flexible on timing. You can find out what major groups are working on and what their priorities are at a given time. If your interests are broad, you'll find it very useful to pick topics that are currently at the top of the government's agenda. Although in some cases it seems like government decisions can take forever, in others, critical choices can happen very fast. If you remain flexible to respond to the government's agenda, presenting alternatives at the right time to the right people can be very successful in changing the course of a government decision.

Specific topics can be anything from demanding an environmental test on a particular location in your neighbourhood to having an impact on Canada's position on a singular vote at the UN. Choosing a specific issue also has advantages. It allows you to focus your time and energy on one concrete task and learn about community organizing first hand. An issue that involves one level of government and a small coalition of community organizations can act as a microcosm of decision-making on a larger scale. Working on everything from raising public awareness to meeting with government officials to dealing with the press can give you good experience that will be helpful with larger advocacy issues later on.

Of course, more often than not, policies tend to find people more than people find policies. The choice of topic may not be yours to make. An issue may have affected you so personally that the choice may have been made for you. If this is the case, it is still a good idea to examine your reasons for wanting to take up a cause. It's going to require persistence and a recognition that it won't be easy. If you understand the deeper reasons for why you are choosing to get involved in the first place, it will be easier to sustain your efforts, learn from your mistakes, and take a long-term view of success.

STEP 2: Identify Your Resources

Ask yourself, "How much time and energy am I willing to give? What specific skills do I have to offer?" In answering this second question, don't sell yourself short. In addition to formal skills gained through your profession, do not discount life skills you may have from years of experience outside a job. Event planning, writing, public speaking, community organizing, and people skills can all be useful when applied in the right situation at the right time. Although you may want to spend your time offering your existing skills to a good cause, your priority may be to learn new ones. Becoming active on a social or political issue is a great way to develop new strengths you never imagined you had.

Another question to ask yourself is this: "Am I looking for a change in career or just a meaningful way to spend some of my volunteer time?" For many, a change in career to a not-for-profit organization is attractive because they are spending their days working for a good cause. Some worry, however, that they do not have the experience necessary to move into a mid- or high-level position that would hopefully keep them roughly on the same pay scale. For professionals, the larger worry is the prospect of a decrease in salary. For those just starting out or interested in pursuing a full career in another field, your objective may be just to get involved in advocacy, without making it your full-time occupation.

As well, volunteering can be difficult when the demands on your time increase as your level of involvement becomes more intense. We all find that when we care about an issue, we can get drawn into devoting many more hours than we originally intended. This can be hard to justify when you have bills to pay and other responsibilities.

Volunteering can be very productive – if you volunteer with a purpose. Rather than taking any volunteer position that is open to you, think carefully about what you want out of your experience aside from the satisfaction of working on an issue that you care about. Spending your free time strategically can help open up options and expose you to new directions that you hadn't considered or imagined. It can also help you to build a whole new set of skills, backed up with experience and a network of new contacts. The best part about volunteering strategically is that you can go directly where you want to. If your goal is to volunteer, you can approach the people you want to work with and the organizations that most fascinate you directly. Offering your services can be the best way into a world that previously seemed inaccessible. In my own case, I had always wanted to work for the United Nations. During university I had the opportunity to intern for an office of the UN High Commission for Refugees in Washington D.C. While the work I did there turned out to be mainly Internet research, being around the office made me aware of a program called Camp Sadako that sent students out for direct experience. Thanks to my volunteer work, the staff knew me and my experience and I was selected to go to Mexico and work with Guatemalan refugees in a refugee camp. This gave me the field experience necessary to complement my academic training, which eventually helped me become qualified for other, larger goals I wanted to pursue. Volunteering for an organization that you believe in will give you an opportunity to learn about the issues it faces. It can also open doors you never knew were closed. When I began volunteering, I had no idea where it would lead, but by strategically choosing an area of focus, my efforts opened up tremendous possibilities I had never thought of.

Many career transitions are fluid – they do not start out with a specific end goal. If you are looking to add a more social, community-oriented dimension to your life, the best way to start is just by exposing yourself to new people, doing new things, and seeing what options become apparent to you.

Examining your reasons for getting involved and volunteering with a purpose will help avoid feeling overworked and underappreciated. It will also give you a new sense of purpose that is directed toward a specific goal.

STEP 3: Find Others

Find others who are working on your issue. Which organizations are involved? Who is for it and who is against it? Beginning with a well-known organization (for instance, the Red Cross or Doctors Without Borders), you can familiarize yourself with who the main actors are and what they are working on. Whether your cause has to do with kids, the environment, health, or an international issue there will be several organizations with valuable experience.

To find a relevant organization, the best place to start is the Web.[2] During your search pay special attention to the organization's mission statement. This will usually offer the best description of what the organization is and what it is about. Some good questions to

---

[2] "For Further Reading" contains a list of good Web sites where you can browse for Canadian charitable organizations by topic.

ask are these: Does it have religious affiliations? Is it connected with one particular political party? How large is the organization? Where is it located? It can also be a good idea to look up any available information on its staff. Note what the group is currently working on. Does it try to cover a broad range of issues or is it focused on a few specific objectives? Many organizations post short bios of at least their executive director, which can give you an idea of where the organization is coming from and their likely approach to tackling an issue. Of course at this stage it will not be possible to be aware of every group working on your topic but you can gain a basic overview of who is doing what.

> "All politics is a battle for public opinion."
> Jack Layton, Leader of the New Democratic Party

STEP 4: Do Some Preliminary Research

Conduct a newspaper clipping search on your topic over the past year or two. Internet searches in newspaper archives by topic will usually give you an overview of how the issue is perceived in the public's eye and what the main areas of controversy are. For those without Internet access, this information is still available through microfiches at your local public library. Some newspapers offer free access to archives, others require a small browsing fee.

Next, find out whether any current government programs address your issue. Departmental Web sites will usually outline all major programs the government is currently running to address an issue. It is crucial to be aware of this material because you want to make sure that what you are proposing will not duplicate existing efforts or recommend actions that have been tried and discounted before. You'll also want reassurance that what you are proposing is better than what currently exists. The only way to get this reassurance is to learn about what is already available and evaluate whether it is effective. To begin your search, go to www.canada.gc.ca to find a list of federal government departments. Programs run by provincial government departments can be found through the home Web site of the province of interest. Be careful not to get lost in too much detail. The goal here is just to help you refine what it is you want to work on and why.

At this stage, it is important to pay close attention to the publicly stated rationale for the government's current program. Government press releases are usually the best source of this information.[3] If you familiarize yourself with the language used to describe your issue, it will help you develop and frame your own arguments later on. As a general example, the Conservative government's press release for the Clean Air Act of 2006 stated that the act demonstrates "a clear commitment to the establishment of short-, medium- and long-term industrial air pollution targets." The key words here are "commitment to establish" rather than simply establishing the targets there and then.

---

[3] Government press releases are available on the Web sites of the relevant departments. Almost all government departments have a link to media resources or announcements by the minister.

STEP 5: Write It Down

Once you have a clearer idea of what it is you want to work on, try to articulate it by pulling your thoughts together on paper under the following headers. At this early stage, the purpose of this document is simply to give you a starting point from which to continue learning about an issue.

The Problem. Begin with the issue you want to address. Try to be as specific as you can about what the issue is and why there is a problem.

> "You must do the groundwork, and you can't do it twenty-four hours beforehand."
> Alex Neve, Secretary General, Amnesty International, Canada

Current Situation. Next focus on what is already being done. Try to describe the major ways the problem is currently being addressed and why you feel this is inadequate.

Proposed Solutions. Outline some thoughts on what you think the solution may be. Pay attention to whether your ideas are similar or different to what is already being done. Next identify one or two organizations that are working along these lines. If none exist, brainstorm ideas of reaching out to individuals and groups who may be interested in starting to work on the issue with you.

Potential Support. Lay out who is likely to support your idea and create a preliminary list of potential allies. Allies may include friends, acquaintances, people with a stake in the issue, or people with influence.

Implications. What would it take to make some of those solutions reality? A good way to develop your ideas is to try to think through the implications of pursuing different solutions at the outset. Would a law need to be changed? Would funding need to shift? Who would be responsible? How could it be done? At this stage, you won't have detailed answers but starting to think through the implications will help give you a sense of where to go next.

STEP 6: Make Connections

Get in touch with those working on your issue by setting up one or two informational meetings. The idea of the initial informational meeting is to supplement your research and help you shape your next step. Aim to leave the meeting with the names and contact information of two additional people who can be helpful to your cause. This is a good way to begin building your own network of contacts. Ideally, if the meeting goes well, the person you are meeting with will offer to connect you to these people personally.

A good place to start is with one or two of the major advocacy organizations you identified. For the most part, individuals working for these organizations will be happy to give you more information about what they are doing and connect you with others working on similar goals.

Another option is to request an informational meeting with the constituency staff of your local member of Parliament (M.P.) or member of your provincial Parliament. Note that

- your federal member of Parliament can be found by entering your postal code or the postal code of your organization at www.electionscanada.ca
- your provincial member of Parliament can be found through the main Web site of your province (e.g., www.alberta.ca)
- your municipal councillors can be found through the main Web site of your city or town (e.g. www.townofantigonish.ca)

"Nothing is short-term. You need patience and determination to get things done."
Senior Official, Privy Council Office

A good M.P.'s office can be very helpful in letting you know what else is going on in your community and who else may be working on your issue. As the representative for your riding, he or she should be keeping track of the issues that are important to constituents. Note that if your purpose is only to gather information, it is probably not necessary to meet with the M.P. himself. While at this early stage you are not likely to see a policy result to your meeting, an informational meeting with your representative's office can be a direct way to link up with a network of people and organizations active on your cause. Once connected, you can focus on finding the right role for you – whether it is raising public awareness, participating in further research, organizing education activities, or working on policy advocacy through direct contact with the government.

In all cases be explicit about what you want from the meeting before you go into it so you can evaluate whether your meeting was successful afterward. Are you looking for specific information? Does the person you are meeting with have a direct connection to a person or organization you would like to get to know? Be sure to come prepared with a list of good questions to ask.

You may end up working with one particular organization that appeals to you. Alternatively, you may end up working as part of a loose coalition of individuals and organizations devoted to the same cause. If your issue is so local that no one is working on it, your first task may be to gather a small group of interested individuals by canvassing and go from there.

Once you have taken these first steps, you are on your way to shaping public policy in this country. While this chapter offers a simple guide on how to start and how to get over that initial feeling of inertia, subsequent chapters will help you refine your ideas, develop a plan, and be strategic about the time and energy you put into your cause. Once you begin, you'll soon discover that it is not difficult. Results are possible – you can have an impact on decisions taken in the future by your government, on your behalf.

"People have more power than they think."
Bill Casey, M.P., Cumberland-Colchester-Musquodoboit Valley

CHAPTER TWO

WHAT DO YOU HAVE TO OFFER?

Building Credibility

In politics, credibility carries a lot of weight. The ability of an advocate, a politician, or a nation to influence the world is strongly tied to their reputation. Political "power" is essentially the ability to influence others to get them to do what you want. This can generally be accomplished in one of three ways: by force, by economic incentive, or by convincing others to adopt your point of view. In political speak, the latter is known as "soft power" or the ability to attract or persuade others so that they *want* what you want.[1]

For advocates, building your reputation requires fostering long-term relationships with both politicians and the bureaucracy. Successful advocates are those

---

[1] Joseph Nye, *Soft Power: The Means to Success in World Politics* (PublicAffairs, 2004).

who have developed these ties while finding a delicate balance between two forces. On the one hand, they are seen as outspoken public critics of the government who legitimately represent the views of their constituency. On the other hand, they are seen as reasonable within government because they offer constructive criticism, backed up by information from reliable sources. Government officials feel they can have candid conversations with these individuals without fear that every view expressed will be leaked to the media and misconstrued.

Knowing when to be confrontational and when to collaborate is a matter of understanding your political capital. In other words, your group should know what you have to offer the government and what the government is looking for from you. Once you understand your value, you can build your credibility and increase your influence on the policies you care about.

The value of outside advice to government has only increased in recent years. Both at home and abroad, democratic governments are finding that they have to do more to bolster their credibility in order to retain the support and confidence of their citizens. Whether we look at massive protests outside international meetings or the U.S. Congress attempting to take back more authority on Iraq, we can see how governments are under pressure to become directly responsive to the citizens whom they seek to serve.

For government politicians in Canada, this means that they are under increasing pressure to include members of Parliament and citizen advocacy groups

"Governments around the world are coming to realize that policies made in secrecy by experts cannot be substantively informed enough, or executed effectively enough, to succeed. More bluntly, we must move beyond secret meetings of experts if policies are to be recognized as legitimate and effective."
Bill Graham, Former Minister of Foreign Affairs and Minister of National Defence

41

in their deliberations on policy development.[2] Rather than working at cross purposes, M.P.s (with their elected legitimacy) and citizens' groups (with their specialized knowledge) are natural allies in working to ensure the government produces policies that people want. Ministers know that their reputations hinge on their ability to sell government policy. They also know they will have a much easier time doing this if they have tested the reaction and responded to important criticisms before the policy is out the door.

Building credibility is as important for nations as it is for politicians or advocates. Even countries with "hard" – economic or military – power are finding that these assets alone are not enough. The United States in Iraq is a case in point. To be truly powerful, a nation must also depend on its soft power – its culture, its values, and its reputation in the rest of the world to achieve the outcomes it desires.

For Canada, soft power, or the power of persuasion, is extremely important. As a country of no more than thirty-one million people, Canada has to work hard to "punch above its weight" in international affairs. In many ways we are very successful. Although

---

[2] There is a question as to the effect that the new Accountability Act of 2006 will have on interaction between the government and civil society. On the one hand, the requirement to log all interactions formally could discourage direct consultation between government officials and citizens' groups. On the other hand, these interactions are now so numerous and so integral to how policy is developed internally, the act could bring greater increased transparency and predictability to the process by which the exchange of information between citizens' groups and government occurs.

there are stronger and richer candidates, we are a member of the G8 and part of central discussions among the world's most powerful leaders. As a developed country without a colonial past, we have fostered a reputation as a humanitarian leader. This reputation is one of our most useful assets. The stronger our reputation and our credibility, the greater the impact we have around the globe.

As an example, let's look at the role Canada played in the global campaign to create the International Criminal Court (ICC). The negotiations and later decision to create an institution with the power to prosecute world leaders on charges of war crimes or crimes against humanity were (and are) extremely delicate. Supporters of despotic leaders did not want to see individuals they consider heroes extradited to an international court that they felt had no business interfering in internal affairs. Powerful countries, like the United States, did not want to cede sovereignty only to see national icons like Henry Kissinger embarrassed in front of the world.[3] From Pinochet in Chile to Slobodan Milosevic in the former Yugoslavia, negotiating the issues surrounding the creation of the court required skilful diplomacy by countries well endowed with soft power.

---

[3] Christopher Hitchens, a writer for *Vanity Fair* and *The Nation*, wrote a controversial book called *The Trial of Henry Kissinger* that argues that former U.S. Secretary of State Henry Kissinger should be brought up on trial for his alleged involvement in the war in Indochina; mass murder in Bangladesh; planned assassinations in Santiago, Nicosia, and Washington D.C.; and genocide in East Timor.

Canada's main means of influencing such a crucial international decision was to rely on our reputation as an "honest broker." During the Rome Conference in July of 1998, Canadian diplomats brokered tactful agreements on the court's most contentious issues.[4] From the definitions of the crimes to the jurisdiction of the court, Canadians were able to bridge gaps and negotiate the compromises that enabled the court to come into existence.

Of course, having an influence on international affairs requires more than a good reputation. But Canada's reliance on its reputation to play a larger role in the world is very useful for advocates. Running a successful campaign here at home can mean tipping the balance in international discussions and having a global impact on the issues you care about. Once the Canadian government had made the ICC a central priority in foreign policy, advocates had a powerful ally in the campaign to see the court universally accepted. Since 1998, rather than working at cross purposes, citizens' groups have worked alongside parliamentarians and the Canadian government to expand the number of countries officially signed on to the International Criminal Court and strengthen the institution so that it can withstand the test of time.

Whether you are working inside or outside the

On the Jubilee Campaign to cancel external debt for the world's poorest countries:

"What was important was the impact that unlocking the issue in Canada had globally."
Dennis Howlett, Make Poverty History Campaign

---

[4] The Statute of the ICC was ultimately adopted at the Rome Conference by a vote of 120 states in favour, 7 against, and 21 abstentions.

system, your credibility largely determines your influence. As a ministerial adviser, I was only as effective as the reputation I built internally. For a department to take direction from a young, "green" aide with few years of government experience, I had to be very careful to try to make sure that I really understood the issues before me, was accurately representing the minister's views, my requests were backed up by a reasonable rationale, and I was able to communicate what I needed effectively.

This chapter will give you some ideas on how to do just that. It begins by identifying your particular assets so that you know your value as a government resource. It then offers some suggestions on how to build your credibility over the longer term so that the government will increasingly look to you for advice. The chapter concludes by looking at ways to strengthen your capacity to act.

IDENTIFY YOUR ASSETS

To be effective it is important that you know what you can offer the government and why they should take you seriously. The better you can understand and articulate your strengths as a group or organization, the more likely it is that the government will recognize your value. Also remember that the government will have some specific objectives in meeting with you. Once you understand what officials are looking for, you can work to build a relationship that is mutually beneficial. What follows is a list of common assets that you may bring to the table.

ASSET 1: *You can offer feedback on what's working and what's not working based on first-hand experience.*

Individuals and organizations can often provide first-hand information to decision-makers on how policies designed in faraway offices actually affect the people who will feel the impact most strongly. Many citizens' groups develop highly specialized knowledge about specific areas of policy based on first-hand experience. Officials in government departments understand that no matter how well intentioned a policy may be, they need to rely on those working in the community for feedback on whether good intentions have led to good results. Even if you are working on a smaller scale, in a local community, you may be in a position to point out unintended consequences of government actions. A new program that distributes blankets to the homeless, for instance, may have an unintended effect. Local community groups that offer people rides to homeless shelters may notice that with the blankets, more people are willing to try to tough it out on the street rather than seek shelter on extremely cold nights. This is invaluable knowledge for officials who want to make sure that their budgets are spent wisely so they can continue to maintain their funding in the future.

This information is valuable not only to officials, but also to politicians. Ministers and M.P.s understand that citizens' groups offer a reality check on policies proposed by government departments. Hearing first-hand from constituents who are affected by these policies gives elected officials a sense of the

> "When groups have solutions born in the trenches, I want to hear them."
> Carolyn Bennett, M.P., St. Paul's, Toronto, Former Minister of State for Public Health

grassroots reaction to departmental recommendations before a final decision is made.

Some organizations may also be able to test new
approaches to meeting the needs of a specific community. Organizations such as Go for Green, for
instance, worked to develop pilot projects with local
schools across Canada to encourage children to get to
and from school safely on their own. Local principals
had noticed that parents were spending more time
driving their kids to school despite the fact that
driving short distances increases greenhouse gases
and reduces the opportunities for kids to get exercise.
To address the issue, local organizations tested new
ways to encourage families to choose biking, walking,
or taking public transportation over driving. The
program was so successful that it was later launched
nationally with funding support from several levels of
government. Because of their local experience, many
groups are well placed to try out alternative solutions
to widespread problems on a small scale. Once an
idea has been "piloted" or tested and evaluated, the
government is more likely to take it on, fund it, or
expand its reach.

ASSET 2: *You may speak for a specific segment of the population and/or have the power to motivate a community to take action on a cause.*

Officials working within government departments
often look to organizations that are independent of
government to provide a channel of communication
into hard-to-reach communities. For example, an

individual or organization may act as a legitimate representative for seniors, disabled persons, or a particular ethnic group. Often the government will rely on these representatives to react to or provide advice on new policy ideas or directions.

If domestic groups are connected with partner organizations in other countries, they can also offer an opportunity for those working abroad to communicate their experience to the government directly. From the government's perspective, these groups offer an additional source of intelligence to inform their actions.

Departmental officials may also meet with community representatives to legitimize their work. If a bureaucrat can present a proposal that has been through local consultations, that proposal will have more legitimacy when it gets to a politician for decision.

Politicians will find this ability to be a "spokesperson" for a particular community even more valuable. Government ministers, M.P.s, and provincial members will meet with representatives of specific communities to gauge the reaction to a policy under consideration. Essentially, these representatives act as a political litmus test for controversial decisions. As a relationship develops, the political offices may stay in close contact with respected representatives to get advice on departmental recommendations and keep informed on how an initiative is received by the public.

"You must represent who you say you do. Misrepresenting yourself will severely damage your credibility."
John Mackay, M.P., Scarborough-Guildwood, Ontario

Similarly, opposition members of Parliament will also meet with community representatives to keep tabs on how their ridings are reacting to specific government policies and where there is cause for criticism. In both cases, however, make sure that you legitimately represent those whom you purport to.

Essentially, the ability to speak with authority for a certain group is a major asset because it gives individuals and organizations leverage with government. This can cause the government to take a second look at the policy before deciding to go ahead. If you also have the ability to mobilize a community to take action, your political value increases. When politicians know there is a direct negative consequence to decisions that they take, they are more likely to listen attentively to concerns in advance.

> **"You have to ask good questions to get good answers."**
> Official, Canadian International Development Agency

ASSET 3: *You can ask good questions.*

Whether you are working through the media, your representatives, or off-the-record meetings with departmental officials, outsiders can raise critical questions to challenge the government's current way of thinking. The best questions are those that cannot be avoided. "But if you create a new landfill in that neighbourhood, how will you prevent kids in the playground across the street from getting sick?"

Many groups choose to put resources into independent research that collects evidence in order to ask good questions of the government. This research can provide government politicians with legitimate questions to ask of their departments before allowing a proposal to go forward. It can also provide opposition members of Parliament with pertinent questions to ask of the government at an opportune time. Outside research can pursue areas unexplored by government departments because of a lack of resources or a lack of interest. The results of such research can force the government to take a second look at a proposed policy and make adjustments as required.

ASSET 4: *When your goals align, you can help the government communicate its message.*

Of course, advocates and the government often disagree. There are times, however, when the broader agendas and common goals coincide. When the government's main objectives align with yours, the government will see you as a potential ally in getting its message across. The government is always looking for positive news. They also know that word of mouth is one of the most powerful ways to generate support. Groups and individuals that benefit from a proposed policy therefore become extremely important as the government moves ahead with implementation.

Advocates in this position hold a valuable card. If you are part of the group that a policy is designed to benefit, the government wants to keep you happy. A policy designed to help single parents, for example, is not going to get good press if a group representing single parents is strongly critical. In policy discussions, the government will be more sensitive to your criticism because they know that if those whom the policy is intended to benefit are unhappy, there is little political point in going ahead. Often, ministers' offices or government officials will try to make an effort to bring these groups into the discussion to help refine the policy to maximize its benefit.

Working with the government in this situation can be very helpful for your group. Specifically, it can build goodwill in your relationship with officials that will always be useful in dealing with later points of tension.

BUILD YOUR CREDIBILITY

Taking advantage of your assets is not always easy. How seriously the government considers your views depends on their perception of your credibility. While you may be well-respected within certain circles or constituencies, it is important to demonstrate that credibility to government officials so they give you the focused attention you deserve.

For government, credibility is based on a number of factors. These include your credentials, expertise, experience, and reputation. If you are advocating on behalf of a group or organization, officials and politicians will ask whether you are seen as a legitimate representative by the community itself. They know that within a group or organization rivalries often exist between different leaders with different points of view claiming to speak for the community as a whole. Before they meet with anyone, government officials will want to assess your reputation based on the views of colleagues who both agree and disagree with your point of view.

Of course, building a reputation based on experience and respect takes time. These things develop over many years of working within a field and gaining expertise. Whether you are just getting started or are well into your advocacy work, you can take a number of steps to be seen as someone who is credible.

Suggestion 1: Know the Ground Rules

The combination of the federal sponsorship scandal of 2004, the Gomery Report of 2006, and the new Accountability Act introduced by the Conservative Party in December of 2006 have made officials and politicians in Ottawa much more nervous about their direct relationships with citizens. In particular, the Accountability Act introduced provisions to toughen the Lobbyist Registration Act, including one that requires all contacts with designated public-office holders to be recorded. While regulations will further define the details, the new law essentially means that advocates are required to officially register as lobbyists and record all activities with senior public office holders such as whom they met, when, and on what particular subject. The government's stated intent with the new legislation is to limit these activities to "prearranged forms of communication" or in-person meetings and telephone calls.[5]

What this means in practice remains to be seen. Clearly the motivation for the law was to reduce abuse

> "It is critical to take an all-party approach. Non-partisan arguments are crucial to your credibility."
>
> Senator Raynell Andreychuk

---

[5] To register as a lobbyist electronically go to strategis.ic.gc.ca, click on "Lobbyists Registration System," and follow the relevant links.

of the system whereby officials in government and lobbyists outside of government could individually profit from trading information informally. The terminology of the Accountability Act is, however, very unfortunate. The term "lobbying" paints a broad negative brushstroke across a whole range of activities that are, and always have been, both necessary and legitimate to the proper functioning of government.

At this point it may be helpful to draw a distinction between lobbying and advocacy as used in this book:

Lobbyists; lobbying: a group of persons who work or conduct a campaign to influence members of a legislature to vote according to the group's special interest.[6]

Note that *to lobby* is primarily defined as *to influence*. To lobby is to sell, to pressure, to persuade, to pull strings, to hype, to solicit, to plug, and to pitch.[7]

Advocate; advocating: to speak or write in favour of; support or urge by argument; recommend publicly.[8]

Here the emphasis is on the notion of *support*. The focus is on the issue or cause. To *advocate* is to argue for, to back, to build up, to defend, to encourage, to recommend, and to justify.[9]

---

[6] *Random House Unabridged 2006 Dictionary* (Random House Inc., 2006).

[7] *Roget's New Millennium Thesaurus, First Edition* (v 1.3.1).

[8] *Random House Unabridged 2006 Dictionary.*

[9] *Roget's New Millennium Thesaurus.*

Remember that advocating to advance your views is both honourable and legal. Politicians and officials in government know that they need to reach out directly to outside sources to both access the specialized knowledge that citizens' groups can offer and ensure that the policies they propose are received as realistic and credible. So despite the current political climate that gives advocacy a bad name, do not be afraid to register as a lobbyist and exercise your right to participate in the decisions that affect you.

Many groups that receive some form of government funding also worry about "biting the hand that feeds them" when getting involved in advocacy. If your organization is a registered charity in Canada, here is a quick list of what charities can and cannot do when it comes to influencing policy decisions. If you or your group is a registered non-profit organization but does not have a charitable number or if you are part of an informal group of citizens working together, these restrictions do not apply.

What charities can do:
- Use 10 per cent of their resources for non-partisan political activities that directly help them accomplish their goals.[10] Non-partisan political activities are those that explicitly call on the public to take a political action. This includes any

---

[10] Within the voluntary sector there are many who feel that this "10 per cent rule" inhibits the ability of charitable organizations to participate in public policy-making and speak out on issues that directly affect those they serve.

appeal to a politician or official to retain, change, or oppose a government law, policy, or decision. It also includes activities to communicate to the public that a law, policy, or decision should be changed, opposed, or retained. Activities to organize, incite, or put pressure on a public official to seek changes are also considered actions that are political in nature.[11]

- Respond to issues raised in election campaigns. During a campaign, charities are free to analyze and comment on proposals directly related to their purpose.
- Raise public awareness. Charities can organize public awareness events provided that the materials they distribute are educational, informative, reasoned, and well-founded.
- Seek support. Charities are permitted to seek the support of elected officials when there is a question of whether a grant is to be made or continued.

What charities cannot do:
- Persuade members of the public to vote for or against a candidate.
- Further the interests of a political party or candidate by distributing literature or organizing activities on their behalf.
- Advocate in support of policies that are not directly related to the corporate purposes of the charity.

---

[11] For a legal definition of political activities visit http://www.cra-arc.gc.ca/tax/charities/policy/cps/cps-022-e.html#P179_17736.

- Participate in political demonstrations on behalf of the charity.
- Conduct a referendum on a political issue.
- Overstep the boundary between education and propaganda (e.g., by providing one-sided information to promote one point of view).
- Finance political activities directly or indirectly.

THE VOLUNTARY SECTOR INITIATIVE (VSI)

The Voluntary Sector Initiative was an undertaking between the federal government and the non-profit/voluntary sector to improve their relationship and strengthen the capacity of the sector to do its work. Between 2000 and 2005 a number of initiatives resulted from the discussion, most notably:

- An accord between the prime minister and representatives of the voluntary sector was signed. The accord establishes values and principles to guide the relationship between citizens' groups and their government.
- Two codes of "good practice" were published. One deals with funding and the other with policy dialogue.
- A Statistics Canada report on the sector contains economic data on the sector for use in further research and planning.

These materials, along with a list of other activities that resulted from the VSI, are available at www.vsi-isbc.org.

The Access to Information Act

While it is widely agreed that after over twenty years in operation, the Access to Information Act needs substantial reform, it remains one of the most valuable tools advocates have for seeking internal information from the government. The act gives Canadian citizens and people present in Canada the right to access information in federal government documents.[12] Individuals may apply to any government department to release information, and departments are under an obligation to comply within specified time limits. Some exemptions under the act allow the government to exclude certain information for reasons of individual privacy, commercial confidentiality, or national security. If your request for access to information is refused, you can complain to the Office of the Information Commissioner. The office acts as an ombudsman with the capacity to investigate complaints and resolve disputes. Similar acts at the provincial level allow for access to provincial government records.[13]

Also note that the Privacy Act gives these same individuals a right of access to certain personal information about themselves and sets out rules and fair

---

[12] The act can be found at http://laws.justice.gc.ca/en/A-1.

[13] To make an application for a specific document, go to the Web site of the relevant department and search for "Access to Information Application." Most departments have their own application that you'll have to fill out. There is a cost to requesting information but the ombudsman accepts complaints from applicants who feel the cost was too high.

practices for the management of personal information by federal institutions.[14]

Suggestion 2: Do Extra Homework

In Chapter 1 I suggested that you do some preliminary research on your topic to get a basic idea of what the government is currently doing to address your issue and how it is generally framed in the media. Now it is time to probe further into your research so that you will be well briefed on the political context in which your advocacy activities will take place.

The groups that are most prepared have the most influence. One of the best ways to build credibility is to show that you are up to date and have done the extra homework before you begin. This doesn't have to take a lot of time and resources if you know where and how to look.

Political Platforms

During elections, political parties publish a variety of policy statements that tell you what commitments the party is willing to make if elected. The Conservative Party's "Stand Up for Canada" or the Liberal "Red Book," for example, are both major policy documents posted on the parties' main Web sites. Before beginning your advocacy efforts, look back to the winning party's platform. See if your issue is mentioned. If it is there, take note of any specific promises

---

[14] More information on the Privacy Act can be found at http://www.laws.justice.gc.ca/en/P-21.

the party made during the election. If not, the document will at least tell you where the government's attention is likely to be focused. Keep in mind, however, that a party platform statement is not government policy. Through expressions of intent such as party resolutions and party platforms, these documents are mainly a means of communicating the party's policy goals to the public. If you can find a link between the government's stated priorities and your own, the platform can serve as a good starting point to argue why your issue is relevant to the government's current agenda.

It can also be useful to look up the platform statements of opposition parties. If other parties have made commitments on your issue, it will give you an indication of how the government is likely to position itself. For the most part, winning parties want to differentiate themselves from the opposition by offering to do more or taking a different approach to a solution for the problem.

> "Politicians have to draw a line between genuine experts and zealots."
> The Right Honourable Joe Clark, Former Prime Minister of Canada

The Speech from the Throne

The Speech from the Throne is the key government policy document to be aware of. The prime minister, working with government departments and the offices of cabinet ministers, uses the speech to outline the government's policy agenda for the current session of Parliament. The speech is read by the governor general to open Parliament and contains the most comprehensive public announcement of the government's intentions.

It is always a good idea to scan the Speech from the Throne to see if your issue is mentioned or if there is an item that is closely related. Government departments look on the speech as the guiding document for all policy memos they wish to bring to the current government for decision. It is viewed as the government's most comprehensive statement of its public commitments.

Departmental officials pay close attention to the language and specific terminology used in the Speech from the Throne. Because officials generally help draft the document, it is written in a way that is considered "actionable" by the bureaucracy. Essentially this means that government departments can then break down the issue for implementation. Many advocates devote significant time and attention to trying to get their language into the Speech from the Throne. A mention of your issue in the speech can be used as a hook to argue for specific action on your issue throughout the current session of Parliament.

Ministerial Speeches

When the governing party appoints a new minister to head a government department, he or she will eventually give a "stump speech" to outline the objectives for their term in office. The minister (or minister's office) will develop stock material and then repeat more or less the same messages at different events.[15]

---

[15] A list of current cabinet ministers is always available on the parliamentary Web site at http://www.parl.gc.ca/information/about/people/key/CurMin.asp?Language=E. Ministerial speeches are posted on the Web sites of their government departments.

Skimming through recent ministerial speeches will give you an idea of where the current minister is coming from. It will also expose you to the specific language used to frame the issues. Knowing what the minister's current priorities are and how they are framed will help you develop effective language to push your issue forward.

Government Policy Statements

It's also helpful to browse any major bureaucratic consultation papers or policy statements that the government has produced. Government "white papers" (documents distributed for public consultation) can be helpful in getting a handle on what the bureaucracy is currently thinking. Policy statements such as the policy statement posted on the Defence department's Web site provide an overview of the bureaucracy's approach to most of the issues under its jurisdiction.[16] All bureaucratic policy papers have to be approved by the ministers and ultimately cabinet so you can read them as statements of official policy.

Suggestion 3: Get to Know Politically Who's Who

Once you have a sense of where your issue fits into the current political agenda, start to make a preliminary list of key politicians who play a role in your cause. Remember that your main sources of access to all politicians and government departments are the

> "Understand the objectives of the government programs you are interested in. The New Horizons Program, for example, is an important program for seniors. These programs change with different ministers so it is important to track speeches and ask specific questions about recent changes."
> Raymonde Folco, M.P. for Laval-Les Îles

---

[16] The full document can be found at http://www.dnd.ca/site/ reports/dps/summary_e.asp.

people you elect to directly represent you: your city counsellor, your member of provincial Parliament, and your federal member of Parliament.

Beyond your local representatives, however, see if other politicians have taken an active interest in your issue in the past. The best way to do this is to browse the biographies of members of the existing parliamentary standing committees that are most likely to discuss your topic.[17] For instance, if your issue has to do with conditions in the workplace, look up members of the Standing Committee on Human Resources and Social Development, the Senate Standing Committee on Social Affairs, or provincial committees such as the Manitoba Standing Committee on Human Resources. Biographies will tell you whether a member is involved in the issue beyond their role on the standing committee and whether they may be interested in meeting with a group outside of their riding.

Alternatively, if you know that a particular politician has been mentioned in the media in connection with your issue, go to their constituency Web site for more information on what they have done and how they have been involved.

Aside from identifying potential friends, it is equally important to identify your potential opposition.

---

[17] A list of federal House and Senate standing committees can be found at www.parl.gc.ca. Provincial standing committees can be found through the main Web sites of provincial parliaments. To find the specific biographies, click on the name of the individual member.

Building an inventory of groups or politicians who are opposed to your issue will help you understand where your criticism will come from and why. It will also give you an idea of the different perspectives that decision-makers will be hearing and the criticisms that those opposed to your point of view will raise.

Suggestion 4: Demonstrate Your Reliability

Politicians and officials working in government will expect you to demonstrate that you are reliable. If you are working informally or as part of an organization, you can ask yourself a number of questions to gauge your ability to demonstrate your credibility in advocating for a cause.

- From what do you draw your information and expertise? Can you point to your education, training, or special skills?
- Can you show that the information on which you have based your point of view is reliable?

If you are working as part of an organization,

- Do you have up-to-date information on your organization?
- Do you have evaluation data describing the impact of your programs and initiatives?
- Do you have a proven track record? Can you point to successful work in the past?

A good way for organizations to demonstrate their reliability is to invite officials and elected representatives to an event to get to know them first-hand. Offer a tour of your organization or invite an official, M.P., or minister to give a speech at a major event. Include policy-makers in your public activities or fundraisers or look for opportunities to have them meet directly with the people doing the work. These types of invitations can be mutually beneficial. Government officials and politicians often welcome the opportunity to get public visibility and be seen as "in touch" with those on the front lines. For organizations, these invitations present a good way to show officials your value, rather than simply telling them about it.

If you are working with just a few others or as part of a loose coalition of more informal groups, it's even more important to demonstrate your reliability. Be careful not to exaggerate your qualifications but also don't sell yourself short. You may have particular experience that makes you well-suited to contribute in a meaningful way to an important policy discussion.

Suggestion 5: Be Aware of Your Reputation

In advocacy, it is especially important to be aware of how you are viewed by your colleagues and adversaries. In a small country, word of mouth travels fast. It is also important to avoid being seen as partisan. If you are too closely allied with a specific political party, it will affect how your ideas are received by politicians and bureaucrats across government. If your principal goal isn't to support one particular political agenda, try to build a reputation based on concern for the issues rather than on how they play out.

Throughout your efforts, be open about your past history and future intentions. If there are issues that have affected your credibility in the past, be ready to acknowledge and correct any misconceptions or assumptions. The Canadian Red Cross tainted blood scandal is a good example. At the outset of every meeting, Red Cross staff would lead with the steps they were taking to remedy the situation. This cleared the air before any meeting began and allowed officials to concentrate on the current issues.

For government, your reputation also depends upon how you handle confidentiality. One way to build confidence is to be clear at the outset of the status of every interaction with a government official, whether he or she is "on the record" or "off the record." If you have an off-the-record meeting, officials are more likely to give you detailed information about what the government is thinking and why. In these types of meetings, you can gain valuable insight into the policy rationale for certain decisions and the types of deliberations going on internally. In meetings that are off the record, officials are more likely to feel comfortable bouncing ideas off you and entering into a serious discussion of possibilities.

Government officials cannot do this if they think or know that you are going to have a press conference after the meeting. Of course, there are times when you will want to use the press to put pressure on the government to bring an issue out into the open. But if officials think this is the primary reason for the meeting or conversation, you will get nothing more than the standard government line. Having a meeting that is "on the record" is entirely legitimate. Just be careful not to give the impression that your sole purpose is to trap the official or politician into saying something that will later be criticized in the press or commit them to something that they are not ready to be committed to. If you are firm that off the record means off the record, you can help build a relationship based on mutual trust.

STRENGTHEN YOUR CAPACITY TO ACT

Chapter 1 looked at assessing your own resources as an individual wanting to get involved. Here, the goal is to focus on individuals working through organizations or coalitions looking to increase the impact of their group's efforts.

Time, Money, and Human Capital

Advocacy requires an initial investment of resources to do the basic homework and design an effective advocacy plan. Once a plan is in place, resources need to be available to monitor progress and make sure you follow through on your strategy. *However, there is no minimum amount of money required to make a difference.* Whether you have a lot of time, money, and human capital or just a little, what matters is not how much but how well you use what you've got.

To strengthen your capacity to act, the first step is to create an accurate picture of what you have to work with. For instance,

- How much time does your group or organization have to devote to advocacy? Do you plan to work on it every day, once a week, once a month?
- Can you afford a full-time or part-time person on the job? How often can you count on volunteers?
- How much do you have to spend on advocacy activities?
- Are you willing to do fundraising for the cause?

When making your initial assessment, don't forget to take into account temporary needs. Are you able to pull in additional paid employees or volunteers on a temporary basis? Assess when and how often you may need extra resources to implement your advocacy plan and how much you need at a bare minimum to keep it going. Think about how to address busy periods in advance so that you can anticipate unexpected costs.

Once you have an accurate picture of the resources at your disposal, you'll be in a better position to choose how to spend those resources wisely. Chapter 6 will discuss the design of an advocacy plan in detail that will allow you to choose activities that will make the most of your available resources.

Unity

A capacity to act is also about a group's ability to build consensus internally so that it can speak with one voice, through a representative who is considered credible. Building consensus involves getting the support of your board, staff, and major volunteers.

If there is serious disagreement on your goals, tactics, or principles, your group will have very little ability to influence government decisions. Issues are often defeated when advocates contradict themselves, bring internal fights out into the open, or convey different messages to the public, politicians, and bureaucrats. If your group or organization has not worked out its causes of tension, it is best to take a step back, have the discussions internally, and wait to act publicly until differences are resolved.

To determine your level of internal consensus, ask yourself the following:

- Have you made key individuals in your organization aware of your plan?
- Has there been opportunity for input?
- Has your final position addressed any major concerns that were raised?

Basic political science tells us that the best way to unify competing forces is to identify a common enemy. Of course, the government is not your enemy, but public division can be. The more you emphasize common goals and objectives, the easier it will be to act as a unified force.

Finally, designate a spokesperson whom people trust. Charisma and public speaking skills are critical. Your spokesperson needs to be able to articulate your goals in clear, simple language. If that person's door is always open or there is a process to voice complaints, others within the organization will feel that their opinions are being heard.

Numbers

In any advocacy campaign, there is strength in numbers. Joining forces with others who share your goals will be both frustrating and rewarding. As most citizens' groups learn early on, finding a consensus within a group of like-minded people is not necessarily easier than finding one with those with whom you disagree. Citizen's groups, non-profit organizations, and individual activists can all have different priorities. There are also inevitable differences in the way they choose to work, when they choose to act, and how hard they want to push.

Be prepared to struggle against the lowest common denominator and work to achieve the broadest possible consensus you can. The best strategy is often to stress the necessity of coming together against outside opposition. While your group may disagree on the details, you may all find common ground in stepping back and looking at the big picture. Being aware of where your political opponents are coming from will help. It will also be easier if the process by which you arrive at your decisions is seen as open, democratic, and fair.

Know that the time to find solutions is before you go public. Failing to build a minimum level of consensus can be extremely damaging to your advocacy efforts. In fact, it can kill all momentum on a hard-won campaign.

Politicians who are confronted with a divided community are less likely to take action because they know that no matter what they do, they cannot win. For example, when Lloyd Axworthy was minister of Foreign Affairs, advocacy groups launched an effort to push Canada to sign on to the Inter-American Convention on Human Rights. While most human rights organizations in the country were in favour of the government signing on, some women's rights groups raised a concern that certain archaic language in the convention would undo hard-won gains on women's issues. Downplaying this division, the campaign got all the way to cabinet. At cabinet when Axworthy presented the issue for decision, other ministers pointed out that signing the convention would not be seen as a victory on human rights, but rather as the Liberal Party backtracking on women's issues.[18]

When governments are confronted with a "damned if you do, damned if you don't" situation, it inevitably results in inaction. Therefore it is crucial to keep the big picture in mind before you decide to go public. Remember that other sectors – such as industry and big business – are very good at speaking with one voice on specific issues when they have to. Although they too have internal divisions and opinions, you can be sure they are working to present a clear and unified position to the government. To help resolve internal divisions in advance, try the following:

---

[18] Canada is still not a signatory to the Inter-American Convention on Human Rights.

- Compare your broad agendas. Identify the larger goals on which you can all agree.
- Compare your specific objectives. Using this chapter as a guide, scale down your goals to a few very specific objectives that garner the widest support.
- Agree on leadership. Choose a representative and allow them to do their job. If the person (or small group) is well respected, they will have greater flexibility to adjust to changes as required.
- Delegate responsibility. Keep everyone involved by assigning specific tasks. The more people have to do, the more they will feel like an active part of the campaign.

You can work with others in a number of ways. You do not have to be formally part of an organization to work together in a way that is mutually beneficial. Are there areas where you can pool resources? A good way to distribute the burden is to appoint a common person to keep others regularly informed about recent ministerial statements, developments in the House of Commons, or articles in the media. One person can track these issues and keep a number of other people up to date.

Another way to work together is to be specific about your plans and see if it's possible to coordinate the timing of your meetings with officials and politicians. This can reinforce your messages and the overall cause. Similarly, there may also be opportunities to pool resources for media events, public awareness activities, or invitations to special events. Most importantly, open a channel of communication so that you can keep track of what others are doing and what progress is being made.

Building a strong coalition is the best way to magnify the impact of your actions. When the government is confronted with a unified and diverse coalition, officials and politicians alike know they have to listen seriously and prepare a good response. Don't be discouraged if a coalition doesn't form overnight. If you care about your issue and build a reputation as a credible resource, others will seek you out to strengthen their voice as well.

CHAPTER THREE

WHAT DO YOU WANT TO ACHIEVE?
Defining Clear Objectives

Many of the big issues of our day are extremely complex. With globalization, an issue that affects one community in one country is linked to other issues in other communities around the globe. In a world that is increasingly interdependent, it can be difficult to narrow down your goals, sort through the issues, and start to think through specific solutions.

Let's look at the issue of Corporate Social Responsibility (CSR) (sometimes called corporate accountability) as an example. Like the environment in the 1980s, CSR is one of the looming issues of the next generation. All over the world, corporations are becoming intricately involved in areas that were traditionally the prerogative of governments alone. Many communities no longer look to government to help build roads, clinics, and schools. In countries where governments

73

are failing to function or never quite extended their reach in the first place, multinational corporations are replacing governments as the major provider of basic services.

Most companies realize that to improve the productivity of their investments they need to help underdeveloped countries build the infrastructure that supports big business. A healthy workforce, a functioning power grid, and a working communications system are all in a company's best interest. If dysfunctional governments are unable or unwilling to provide these services, companies can't wait. Whether they like it or not, many corporations find themselves wading into areas that can and do have complicated social and cultural repercussions.

But why does it matter who delivers these services as long as the people get them? The big difference is that when governments (particularly democratic ones) are responsible for providing access to clean water and health care, they are accountable to the laws and regulations designed and approved by elected representatives of the people. Corporations, on the other hand, currently have no binding legal structure to govern their actions in community development.

On some issues, the waters become very murky. When companies start to create private security forces to protect their assets, for instance, a whole host of serious issues can arise. While recruiting and training local members of the community can provide jobs, it can also tip a delicate balance of power in an internal conflict and cause an array of unforeseen consequences. In the worst-case scenario, something as simple as providing new jobs can increase divisions based on class or race, fuel ethnic tensions, and lead to an escalation of conflict or all-out war.

Currently the international approach to these issues is to encourage companies to voluntarily comply with accepted ethical standards as set out in several published guidelines on "corporate social responsibility." More and more, however, pressure is mounting to start looking at the questions of whether and how to regulate giant multinational corporations that, in many cases, have more power and money than national governments in the countries where they do business.

Putting laws in place is by no means easy.[1] Many countries where the serious problems are occurring have weak judicial systems and underdeveloped infrastructure to assist gathering evidence and mounting investigations. In these places, national governments are, at best, unwilling or, at worst, outwardly obstructionist when it comes to investigating a case against a multinational corporation that has brought capital and jobs to a struggling economy. Add to that the

---

[1] The case of the class action suit against Talisman Energy operating in Sudan is a good example. The suit alleged that Talisman was complicit with the Sudanese government's human rights abuses against non-Muslim Sudanese living in the area of Talisman's oil concession in the south and that these abuses amounted to genocide. The case was recently dismissed because of a lack of sufficient evidence. The plaintiffs are considering whether to appeal the dismissal. For more details, go to Business and Human Rights Resource Centre at http://www.business-humanrights.org/Categories/Lawlawsuits/Lawsuitsregulatoryaction/LawsuitsSelectedcases/TalismanlawsuitreSudan.

challenge of building the capacity to monitor and enforce new laws and you have an advocacy campaign to span a generation.

So where does it start? Too many people give up on political activism too early. Either they don't see a result to their efforts fast enough, or they become discouraged at the sheer size of the task before them. But this doesn't have to be the case. One of the most important causes for this frustration is a failure to define clear objectives. When your advocacy objectives are not clear, it is impossible to form realistic expectations about the results you want to achieve. More than any other factor, confused objectives can lead to dissatisfaction because neither you nor the decision-maker can come to an understanding of what constitutes success or how progress can be measured.

Once you've chosen the issue you want to work on and sketched out a preliminary idea of what's involved, it's time to focus on defining clearer objectives.[2] The goal of advocacy is to enable outside actors to gain access to, and have a voice in, the decision-making of government institutions. In the longer term, advocacy also seeks to change the power relationships between these institutions and the people affected by their decisions to ultimately change the institutions themselves and bring a clear improvement to people's lives.[3] One of the most common mistakes

---

[2] See Chapter 8 on creating a rough draft of a one-page brief.

[3] David Cohen, Rosa de la Vega, and Gabrielle Watson, *Advocacy and Social Justice: A Global Action and Reflection Guide* (Kumarian Press, 2001), Chapter One.

people make in tackling these complex issues is to confuse two major objectives of advocacy: to raise awareness and to change policy. Both are absolutely necessary to achieving results, but each leads to different means and ends. Although these goals are not mutually exclusive – in fact, some of the most effective individuals and organizations pursue both at once – you need to be clear about which goal you are pursuing with every action you take.

When you are making recommendations to government, it is especially important to be deliberate about your objectives. The language you choose to express your recommendations is extremely important. This chapter will discuss the two approaches so that your actions in pursuit of one goal can support the achievement of the other. The last section offers a step-by-step guide to developing recommendations to government that will lead to satisfying results.

> "Basically, there are two types of campaigns: one for issues already on the agenda, and one for issues you want to get on the agenda."
> Kristen Ostling, Canadian Council for International Cooperation

PUBLIC AWARENESS CAMPAIGNS: NO NEGOTIATION

Social movements are not carried forward just by moderates. Radicals who make no compromises are the ones who set the bar high and push society to accept alternative ideas as a new norm.[4] Public awareness campaigns combined with public engagement – or motivating the public to take some action toward a

---

[4] Once again I want to emphasize the difference between a "radical" and an "extremist." "Radicalism" refers to going to the root or origin of a problem and favouring drastic change from accepted or traditional norms. "Extremism" refers to uncompromising adherence to a particular political or religious ideological position.

specific cause – are critical to achieving long-term social change.

If your objective is to change the way people think or influence what they do, a public awareness campaign will be your main advocacy tool. You choose this route when your goal is to educate, engage the public, and garner support for your cause.

A major advantage of choosing to work on your issue by getting involved in a public awareness campaign is that the time you devote to your cause can be flexible and even sporadic. You can get heavily involved in one event for a short period of time or moderately involved in a steady campaign for many years.

> **"Politicians don't create the bandwagon, they jump on it."**
> Liz Mulholland,
> Former Adviser, Prime Minister's Office

Raising public awareness is about challenging a cultural norm or introducing a new perspective on a widely held belief. If your purpose is to raise public awareness, you don't have to compromise. What's important is to get a new message out that emphasizes clear principles based on common values. Once again, the language you use is very important. For example, the message of your campaign may be "Refugees are not criminals. They should not be detained without charge."

Here, your goal is not necessarily to see a specific policy change. You do not deal with the complex questions of how to determine who is a refugee or what to do if there is well-founded intelligence that a person could pose a serious danger to the public. You are not offering a solution to a complex question of public policy. Rather, you are trying to reach as many people as possible in hopes of building a broad constituency of support for this particular point of view.

Public awareness campaigns with a radical message can be very effective. The campaign to demolish the World Bank and the IMF (International Monetary Fund) is a great example. Critics from both the left and the right argued that both institutions were promoting and following a fundamentally flawed development model. To ensure debt repayment, the IMF and the World Bank required countries to cut spending on education and health, eliminate food and transportation subsidies, privatize national assets, and freeze wages. By prioritizing exports, countries forced their farmers to shift from growing food for local consumption to producing export crops destined for wealthy nations. The result is an increase in poverty, a reduction in a government's ability to develop a strong domestic economy, and an opportunity for unscrupulous corporations to exploit workers and the environment.

Critics ran a public awareness campaign with a clear message: these institutions and their policies are so flawed that when it comes to alleviating poverty, they make things worse, not better. Although the campaign failed in dismantling the institutions, it was very successful in accomplishing its public awareness goal. The idea that the World Bank and the IMF are flawed institutions is now widely held. The campaign succeeded in turning public opinion against the institutions, exerting enough pressure and laying the groundwork for a desired need for change. Ordinary people, across many walks of life in many countries, got the message and even the top officials within the bank now recognize the need to implement a substantial and continual process of reform.

Although public awareness campaigns can lead to shifting attitudes and a gradual change in public consciousness, before you choose to work on one, it is critical to be aware of their limits. Public awareness campaigns rarely lead to short-term results. The specific message of the campaign is almost never transformed into actual government policy. While such campaigns may succeed in shutting down a meeting or slowing government action in an unwanted direction, it is difficult for them to translate into an immediate change in policy. Generally the messages are not specific enough, they do not take into account government constraints, and they do not deal with issues of how to actually make it happen.

Here is an example of an original recommendation presented by a coalition of activists working on human rights in Colombia:

> Canada should support and accompany human rights defenders and encourage an independent, strong and diverse human rights community in Colombia.[5]

When ministers or officials are confronted with this type of recommendation, they will most likely

"Public awareness is important for making a complex issue understandable to people."
Dennis Howlett, Make Poverty History Campaign

---

[5] Draft recommendation presented by the Americas Policy Group of the Canadian Council for International Cooperation.

agree in principle, but will not see any concrete follow-up action. The common response would be "We share this goal and here is a list of what the government is already doing to support human rights in the country." In this scenario advocates are left frustrated that nothing new will be done, and government officials are left with the impression that no matter how much they do, it will never be enough.

If your goal is to raise awareness of an issue, the first step is to decide who your target audience is. If it is the public, good public awareness campaigns usually include a substantial element of public education. In this case, for example, a public awareness campaign could use something like this:

> Human rights defenders are under siege in Colombia. Under the new Democratic Security Policy, activists have been equated with "defenders of terrorism" and reports of human right violations by the military have increased, including extra-judicial executions and torture. Canada must do more to protect human rights defenders in Colombia.

Here the goal is to reach as many people as possible. Success can be measured by how many people are aware of the issue, how many support the cause, and whether that number has increased. Success could mean that more M.P.s are motivated to speak out on your specific cause. Keep in mind that governments conduct public opinion polls regularly. They are looking to identify which issues are important to the public and why. The more awareness you can build, the more likely it is that the government itself will pick up on the necessity of dealing with your issue. If polling consistently shows that a certain issue is important to the public, the government will want to respond. A case in point is the Harper government's shift on global warming. Although the issue was not at the top of the government's agenda, consistent polling results showed that failing to address the issue was severely affecting Harper's approval rating and led the government to make climate change a new priority.

Public awareness campaigns can also be successful when they do not take a radical position. In particular, campaigns can be useful in helping to build coalitions of different groups that may come together around a common cause. A successful campaign will help you identify partners, build relationships, and make the public aware that there is a movement in favour of a general change in the government's long-standing policy direction.

The gun control campaign in Canada is a good example. Following the shooting of twenty-eight women at l'Ecole Polytechnique in Montreal in December 1989, a diverse group of interested citizens began to work on a comprehensive approach to gun control. The group included a professor at Ryerson University, a Metropolitan Toronto police officer, the executive director of the Ontario Provincial Police Association, a criminologist, representatives of women's organizations, and student activists from the school itself. This group formed the nucleus of what grew into Canadians for Gun Control. Within government, the Liberal caucus was divided so groups had to nuance their positions to try to get a majority of members of Parliament on side. The pro-control side was successful in prodding the government to take action largely because it built such a broad coalition of diverse members who came to a consensus on the middle ground. When women's groups work alongside police associations, members of all political parties, urban and rural community groups, and organizations that have both national and regional appeal, their cause becomes difficult to ignore. When a diverse coalition launches a public campaign with a clear message, governments know they need to respond.

Campaigns do not have to be international or even national to be successful. When you work through the media, local community issues can become so sensitive politically that the provincial or federal governments have no choice but to intervene. A good public awareness campaign can make even local issues a top priority for the government that demands a response.

> "To build a public campaign is to till the soil."
> Jack Layton, Leader of the New Democratic Party

POLICY ADVOCACY: DEMOCRATIC COMPROMISE

While public awareness and policy advocacy are certainly related, this book focuses on policy advocacy, or techniques to affect specific government decisions. Whether you want to continue, discontinue, change, or introduce a new government policy, the focus of policy advocacy is to see a specific result. That result, however, may not be exactly as you intended. Changing policy will never be easy. Unlike a public awareness campaign, it requires compromise and negotiation. It also requires the difficult task of looking at your issue from opposing points of view and proposing solutions that take into account real government constraints. Choosing to enter into negotiations on what you hope to achieve will usually mean that your recommendations will not be adopted exactly as you proposed them.

The reality is that government decision-making is about finding an acceptable balance between competing interests. Although there are times when government can and should take a leap of faith and lead on an issue despite fierce opposition from one side, this is not an option for the majority of government decisions. For a decision to be legitimate and sustainable, it must have a minimum degree of support from all those with a major stake in the outcome, even though they may come from very different points of view.

Working as an adviser on human rights to the minister of Citizenship and Immigration, I was involved in the discussions to develop the new Immigration and Refugee Protection Act, which was adopted as law in 2002. How decision-making works was eye-opening for me.

Most decisions on immigration policy are about finding a balance between two extremes. If you close

"Don't let your desire for perfection get in the way of progress."
The Honourable Elinor Caplan, Former Minister of National Revenue, Minister of Citizenship and Immigration, and Ontario Minister of Health

the door too tightly, legitimate people will be denied access to the country; if you open the door too wide, those who would abuse the system can slip through. We called this the "Osama bin Laden vs. Nelson Mandela dilemma." If we took a zero-tolerance policy that forbid anyone with a criminal record from applying to enter the country, Nelson Mandela, with his history as a political prisoner during the apartheid era, would be denied. But if we mandated that only those with verifiable criminal records would be denied, Osama bin Laden, who has never been convicted of any crime, would have to be allowed entry. To make an informed decision on any immigration policy proposal, you have to look at an issue from at least three fundamental perspectives. How would this policy affect a legitimate immigrant? How would it affect a genuine refugee? And finally, how could someone who wants to abuse either system use this policy to enter or stay in Canada illegally?

One issue, for example, was the question of barring access to Canada to those who are fugitives from justice. At first glance, this seems like a straightforward decision. Canada does not want to be a safe haven for criminals, so it follows that Canada should prevent fugitives from entering the country. Once you look at it from the perspective of a refugee, however, the issue becomes more complicated. Genuine refugees could have a well-founded fear of persecution based on their political opinion. If the refugees are victims of state persecution, they could be considered a "fugitive from justice" by an oppressive regime. Therefore, it follows that a good policy would spell out that "fugitive from justice" should refer only to jurisdictions that are recognized as having internationally acceptable standards. Then again, let's look at this from an enforcement perspective. If you define "internationally acceptable standards" too narrowly, serious criminals will use this policy as a loophole to enter the country.

Clearly, to arrive at the right balance, a minister needs several voices arguing from very different points of view. The only way for this to happen is to have informed citizen participation in policy-making. Joining forces with like-minded people and working in an organizational structure that makes the most sense for you is the best way to get your message across. Policy advocacy can give you a sense of satisfaction and real progress, but it will not lead to dramatic change overnight. Choosing to go after a specific change in policy can be far more involved and more time consuming than getting involved in a public awareness campaign. It requires thorough preparation and a commitment to follow through. But if you are strategic about what you push for and how you spend your time, you'll find it extremely satisfying to see your views reflected in final government decisions.

SMART Objectives

If your goal is to change policy, your recommendations will be effective if you follow the widely used SMART guidelines for developing clear objectives.

SMART objectives are those that are specific, measurable, achievable, realistic, and time-bound.

Let's look at a worst-case example. At Foreign Affairs, some groups would spend precious time and resources on setting up a meeting with the minister only to present recommendations that were vague or too general, with no clear objective or way to follow up such as "Minister, increase Canada's focus on human rights when dealing with the United States."

From a minister's perspective, this sort of meeting is destined to have little impact. It is unclear what the specific "ask" is or what the group is expecting the minister to do. The minister is likely to leave the meeting frustrated because there is no clear way to attempt to satisfy the demand, and the group is bound to leave frustrated because they will not see any clear progress.

By contrast, a SMART objective would be framed along these lines: "Minister, will you put the treatment of prisoners in U.S. custody on the agenda of every high-level Canada-U.S. meeting in the next six months?"

In this case, the issue is specific and the request is measurable. Practically speaking, this would mean that for an upcoming G8 meeting, there is an explicit request to put a particular issue on the agenda for a meeting between the prime minister and the president. For the next foreign ministers' meeting, there is a direct request to put it on the agenda of the Canadian foreign minister and the U.S. secretary of state. At the next meeting between security agencies, there is a request to raise it between our minister of Public Safety and the director of Homeland Security.

With the SMART objective, the minister now can work on a satisfying response. He or she may say, "We can't raise it in the one meeting but we can and will raise it in the other two." The goal is self-evident and the response to the request can be measured in concrete terms.

How can you develop recommendations to government that are clear? The following offers a step-by-step guide to defining your objectives and framing your policy recommendations. I have used the example of the same policy recommendation throughout to illustrate each step.

STEP 1: Brainstorm (Why, What)

In Chapter 1 we discussed drafting a rough copy of a briefing note that will eventually become a very important tool in your advocacy campaign. Going back to that draft, it is now time to develop your objectives in more detail. Take a second look at how you described the problem and your initial suggestions for the solution you would like to see. Start to brainstorm further ideas on what the crux of the problem is and how you think it can best be addressed. The goal of the brainstorming phase is to develop a draft statement in the form of a recommendation to government.

Looking at our previous example from a Canadian civil society organization, the initial draft of a policy recommendation looked like this:

Canada should support and accompany human rights defenders and encourage an independent, strong, and diverse human rights community in Colombia.

At this stage, the purpose is to develop your ideas on paper in as much detail as possible.

STEP 2: Analyze Your Recommendations

Take a critical look at your draft recommendation and ask yourself some specific questions.

What Is the Specific "Ask"?

What kind of support are you asking for? In this case, it is most likely that the request is for diplomatic and/or financial support.

The draft uses the word "accompany," but accompany how? Is the request to have Canadian government officials physically present? When? Under what circumstances? If you do not have a clear idea of what you mean by a word, consider whether it is necessary.

Is this draft as specific as it can be? Are there any other concrete tasks that can be suggested to the government? The same group also had other specific recommendations on how the government can "encourage a strong and diverse human rights community." These included working with certain women's organizations and looking for opportunities to help particularly vulnerable groups. As much as possible, include such specific tasks here so that the government knows what it is being asked to do.

Why Are You Making This Request?

The reasons for your request may be expanded into a supplemental policy brief but they should also be apparent in your recommendation. Ideally, your recommendations should be able to stand on their own so that they are clear at the outset to M.P.s, ministers, or officials.

The reason we should support human rights defenders is explained in the latter part of the recommendation: to encourage an independent, strong, and diverse human rights community.

To make a direct impact, the "why" should link to goals that the government holds with you. As much as possible, frame the "why" in the language of stated government objectives. Here we see the importance of language once again. Ministerial speeches, government Web sites, and the Speech from the Throne all contain catch phrases for the goals the government is trying to achieve. The more you can align your objectives with those the government has stated as a priority, the better the chance of drawing greater government attention to the issue.

Who Is the Recommendation Directed At?

For the public, recommendations can be put to something as general as "Canada." For specific meetings, however, it is useful to break them down by who has the authority to carry out the action. In this case, Foreign Affairs would have the authority and capability to provide diplomatic support to human rights defenders, and the Canadian International Development Agency would be responsible for supporting them financially.

In this example, "human rights defenders" is also quite vague. Which people are you talking about? Particular organizations or individuals? If possible, help officials to break down who exactly the recommendation is directed at.

How Can It Be Done?

For your objective to be fulfilled, what specific kind of change is required?

- Legislative change – requires an amendment to an existing law through parliamentary review.
- Regulatory change – requires a change to a government regulation. Regulations are drafted by government departments and do not go to Parliament for consideration.
- Political policy change – requires a decision at the cabinet level to change a government policy.
- Departmental policy change – requires a change in the guidelines given to officials who make decisions based on delegated authority.

Finally, are you requesting a change in a funding decision or direction? Whatever your answers, it is important that you keep in mind the mechanism by which change can be achieved.

STEP 3: Revise Your Recommendations According to SMART Criteria

Once you have analyzed and revised your draft recommendation, you are ready to test it against SMART criteria. Going back to our example, your revision may now look like this:

> Canada should provide diplomatic and financial support to human rights defenders in order to encourage an independent, strong, and diverse human rights community in Colombia. Specifically, Foreign Affairs (DFA) and the Canadian International Development Agency (CIDA) should
>
> • Maintain or increase political and financial support to women's organizations that are working to defend women's human rights and to build policy alternatives to defend women's human rights.
> • Seek out opportunities to address the particular needs of vulnerable groups of displaced people: women and their children, indigenous peoples, and Afro-Colombians.

Once you have a revised recommendation, you can now test it against each SMART criterion.

Specific

For an objective to be specific it should refer to an action or behaviour that can be observed. It may be linked to a rate, a percentage, or a frequency. Use words that denote a concrete action to describe your goal. In this example, the request is now very clear and a rate or percentage is not necessary. Specific departments are asked to do things that are within their power to do.

Measurable

How can you monitor or track the behaviour or action? What evidence do you need to confirm that a change has occurred? Your objective may include a numeric or descriptive goal. For example, it is not just that we want to increase X, but we want to increase X by a said amount.

Here, the request is for a concrete action that can be observed and measured. One can compare the number of ministerial (or ambassador) statements or the level of financial support from one year to the next.

Achievable

For your policy objective to be achievable, there should be a likelihood of success. In contrast to a public awareness objective, which does not need to be limited, your policy objective should be adequately limited in scope so that it is *feasible*. This doesn't mean that it will be easy or simple to achieve your goal, just that it is possible to make progress.

In the above example, the request is not unlimited in scope, therefore it is possible to achieve. CIDA and DFAIT (Department of Foreign Affairs and International Trade) already provide some support to these causes within available resources, so it is not out of the question for them to continue to provide the same or an increased level of support.

Realistic

Your objective should reflect available resources, or resources that you can work on acquiring. Also try to make sure that the objective is actually relevant to you or your organization. Does it fit within your mandate? Is it within your capacity to affect change on this particular issue?

Here, beyond the need for resources to present the recommendation, there may also be a need for resources to monitor and track follow-up. If the recommendation is within your mandate and those resources are in place, the recommendation is realistic for you.

Time-bound

Your objective may set a clear start and/or end date for the actions you desire. It may also include interim steps that are needed to plan and make incremental progress.

A time frame may or may not be necessary, depending on your recommendation.[6] In our example, if desired, a caveat could be added, ". . . before the next meeting of the Organization of the American States."

STEP 4: Organize Your Objectives

The most common mistake advocates make is presenting a recommendation that is beyond the scope of the power of the person receiving the request. This

---

[6] Refer to Chapter 6 on creating a timeline.

is where departments will "pass the buck" indefinitely because they do not know what to do with it. Once you've finalized the wording on your recommendations, organize your objectives according to whom they are directed at. Direct specific recommendations to the appropriate decision-maker:

- Officials within specific departments
- Ministers of specific departments[7]
- Members of Parliament

This will help you later decide which advocacy activities to choose and how to use your time and energy wisely. For instance, members of Parliament do not have much say in how to frame Canada's diplomatic messages to other countries. Therefore, in this example, your time and energy would be better spent meeting with officials from the Department of Foreign Affairs, the Canadian International Development Agency, and their relevant ministers if possible.

STEP 5: Prioritize

If you have several goals, be sure to prioritize them. Although you may develop as many recommendations as you wish, be sure to prioritize which are the most important to you. You don't want to confuse the person you are meeting with, nor do you want to take attention away from your primary goal.

---

[7] How to identify the appropriate decision-maker is covered in more detail in Chapter 4, "What Do You Need to Know?"

For all advocacy activities, you will want to know which recommendations are your top three so that you can leave people with a clear idea of what you want.

If your goal is to change a specific policy, success will not mean having your view adopted exactly as you proposed it. For our purposes, successful advocacy is about making sure that your information is

"Indicate what your absolute top priorities are. If you make ten recommendations, stress the top three."

Anita Neville, M.P., Winnipeg South Centre

TIPS FOR DEFINING GOOD RECOMMENDATIONS

Make sure that your recommendations fit within stated government priorities. Although you may want to change these priorities in the longer term, your specific recommendations should be politically relevant now. You can achieve this by making sure that your "ask" fits with the current government agenda.

Avoid jargon or rhetoric that is specific to your organization or your field. In particular, watch out for buzz words that can be interpreted in several ways or refer to a state of mind. For example, words such as "sensitize" or "empower" are difficult for those in government to work with. These may be important larger, longer-term goals, but in designing your advocacy strategy, they can be abstract and difficult to measure. In relations with the government, such words largely have no meaning and tend to lose attention fast because nobody knows quite what to do with them. On funding applications in particular, these types of words make a proposal very difficult to justify from a bureaucratic point of view and may be rejected for lack of specificity.

Finally, test out your objectives by asking for some outside reads, by people who come from a variety of perspectives. This will help you to know whether the language you are using is clear and accessible.

before the right person, at the right time, in the right place. This means that at every stage of decision-making, your point of view will be well presented, seriously considered, and reflected in the final decision taken by the government. This book is urging you to become a policy activist. Advocacy is a fight not just for new options, but for new language and a new mindset to frame the issues that are up for discussion before decision-makers. If your objectives are clear and your interventions strategic, you can have a direct impact on a government decision that affects you.

CHAPTER FOUR

WHAT DO YOU NEED TO KNOW?

How Government Works
and How Decisions Get Made

The goal of this chapter is to give you a basic idea of how government works and how decisions get made. Understanding who is in charge, what the lines of command are, and how the pieces fit together will help you decide how and when to make your arguments so they have the best chance of being heard.

Some would argue that the task itself is impossible. Policy development is complex and not always logical. Individual personalities can play either a refreshing or infuriating role. Daily events in politics or the media cause plans to change and exceptions to be made. For anyone trying to influence a decision from the outside, it seems that decision-making can range from being totally overly regulated – with minor details going up each level of a massive hierarchy at an agonizing pace – to completely messy, with dramatic changes being made through hushed, last-minute hallway conversations in the midst of near chaos.

This chapter breaks down the structure of government and the policy process into logical steps for clarity. In doing so, it risks presenting an ideal version of how things work that may not reflect some of the common, unfortunate, and illogical obstacles that one can run into. Even in government, however, the exceptions are not the norm. All issues usually go through a basic process before a decision is made. Getting a handle on this process will make you familiar with the way things are supposed to work. It will put you on par with those on the "inside" who have a clearer idea of what to expect when following the development of a government decision. When it comes to hitting a real wall – an insurmountable obstacle or an impossible personality – the best strategy is always to create an advocacy plan that is not dependent on one course of action alone.

Part I starts with a brief overview about how our system of "responsible government" is structured. It then includes a short description of who does what – from the governor general, the cabinet, the prime minister, and the Privy Council office to government ministers and government departments. How Parliament works will be covered through a discussion of the House of Commons, the Senate, the role of the Opposition, and how a bill becomes a law.[1] Part II

---

[1] For more information on a particular aspect of the government, refer to "For Further Reading" for a list of good resources.

then turns to how decisions get made. It looks at the general stages of the policy process, then three fundamental questions you need to ask to move your issue forward: Who is the actual decision-maker? Who influences the decision? How will it be implemented? The chapter concludes with some tips to help you have an impact on particular types of decisions.

I. RESPONSIBLE GOVERNMENT

Canada's model of democracy is characterized by two basic principles: responsible government and representative government. Responsible government essentially means that the executive branch of government is responsible to the legislative one. The executive branch includes the prime minister, the appointed ministers that make up the cabinet, and the departments of the civil service that support them. As long as

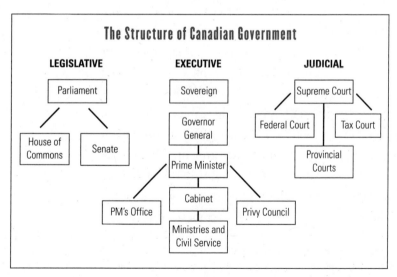

The Structure of Canadian Government

LEGISLATIVE	EXECUTIVE	JUDICIAL
Parliament	Sovereign	Supreme Court
House of Commons Senate	Governor General	Federal Court Tax Court
PM's Office	Prime Minister	Provincial Courts
	Cabinet Privy Council	
	Ministries and Civil Service	

the executive retains the confidence of Parliament, it can continue to govern. If it loses the confidence of Parliament – or a vote of non-confidence is passed in the House of Commons – the government has to resign and call a general election.

In our system, the prime minister and the cabinet are responsible for the overall management and direction of the government. This includes developing and setting policy; raising and spending revenue; administering and applying the law; and even invoking the War Measures Act, which suspends all normal civil liberties and rights.[2]

The enormous centralized powers of the executive are safeguarded against abuse through accountability to Parliament. Parliament is our central representative institution. Every Canadian is directly represented in the House of Commons through an elected member of Parliament. As C.E.S. Franks describes in *The Parliament of Canada*, Parliament has four essential functions:

- To establish a legitimate government through the electoral process.
- To make government work (give authority for funds to govern the country).
- To make government behave (act as a watchdog on executive authority).

---

[2] C.E.S. Franks, *The Parliament of Canada* (University of Toronto Press, 1987).

- To make an alternative government (let the opposition parties present their case to the public and offer a credible choice to replace the party in power).

It is important to note that Parliament does not play a dominant role in making policy. Parliament's role in legislation and producing resolutions or committee reports is largely directed at scrutinizing what the government does rather than formulating policy.

WHO DOES WHAT[3]

The Governor General and Lieutenant-Governors

Canada is described as a parliamentary democracy and a constitutional monarchy. This means that the Queen of England is still our de facto head of state. The governor general is the Queen's representative in Canada. She is therefore considered one of the three branches of our constitutional monarchy, which includes the House of Commons, the Senate, and the governor general. In Canada there is a clear separation between the role of the head of state (who is appointed by the Queen on the advice of the prime minister) and the head of government (who is the prime minister, an elected representative). The governor general's main roles are

---

3 Canada*info* Web site at http://www.craigmarlatt.com/canada/images&downloads/downloads_govt.html.

- To give royal assent to a bill once it has passed through the House of Commons and the Senate.
- To officially summon and dissolve Parliament.
- To deliver the Speech from the Throne outlining the government's policy objectives and plans for legislation (given at the opening of Parliament).
- To sign state documents such as orders-in-council, commissions, and pardons.
- To host visiting heads of state.
- To preside over the swearing in of the prime minister, the chief justice, cabinet ministers, and members of the Privy Council.

At the provincial level, the monarch is represented by the lieutenant-governor. The role of the lieutenant-governor in each province mirrors that held by the governor general at the federal level. Like the governor general, the lieutenant-governor summons, prorogues (postpones), and dissolves the legislature and reads the Speech from the Throne at the opening of each session. With the advice of the premier, he or she appoints and swears in members of the executive council (or cabinet).

The monarch, governor general, and lieutenant-governors are offices created by the Canadian Constitution. The structure of their offices and their role in government cannot be altered without the unanimous approval of all provincial legislative assemblies, along with the Senate and the House of Commons in Ottawa.

The Cabinet

The cabinet is the central executive decision-making body of both the federal and provincial governments. Cabinet is divided into several committees that each preside over a particular set of issues. The prime minister is ultimately responsible for which ministers sit on each committee and which issues they are to address. Cabinet committees are convened on various topics such as economic affairs, foreign affairs, and national security. At the provincial level, cabinet is structured in much the same way under the authority of the provincial premier.

Some of the cabinet's specific responsibilities are

- To propose new laws by approving departmental drafts of government bills.
- To introduce government bills into the legislature.
- To approve major policy and spending decisions for all government departments.
- To develop and propose the budget.
- To approve all governor-in-council appointments to Crown corporations, agencies, boards, and commissions. This covers a range of positions from appointments to head the Bank of Canada and VIA Rail to positions on the Canada Council for the Arts.

The Prime Minister (PM) and the Prime Minister's Office (PMO)

The prime minister heads the executive branch of government and oversees all meetings of the full cabinet. He or she is responsible for appointing cabinet ministers, senators, the chief justice of Canada, the governor general, and the lieutenant-governors of the provinces. The PM is also responsible for the timing of the resolution and the dissolution of Parliament.[4]

The size and content of the Prime Minister's Office will vary depending on who is in power. The specific titles of the positions will also change with a change in government. In general, however, the term "Special Assistant" or "Policy Adviser" indicates that a person is a member of the prime minister's personal political staff. A Prime Minister's Office will usually include the following:

- A chief of staff. He or she is the prime minister's right-hand person who runs the PMO, hires staff, oversees the PM's schedule, and coordinates the flow of material on and off the prime minister's desk.
- A social policy adviser (and team). They form a small unit to drive the social policy agenda of the PM. They also follow or get involved in any contentious social policy issues initiated by other departments.
- An economic adviser (and team). They oversee the economic and fiscal agenda of the PM and closely follow the activities of the Finance Department.
- A foreign policy/national security adviser (and team). They will work closely with the departments

---

[4] John Bejermi, *How Parliament Works* (Borealis Press, 1996).

and ministers of Foreign Affairs and Border Security but will often offer independent advice to the PM.

- Regional political advisers. The PM will usually have a special assistant for each region of the country. The special assistant for Ontario, for example, will follow the political developments in Ontario, handle concerns from Ontario M.P.s, and act as a caucus liaison.

- A director of communications or press secretary. The PM has his or her own communications unit to deal with all interaction with the media.

- A director of appointments. This person and their staff will review applications for key appointments and provide political advice to the PM on which candidates should fill particular positions.

- A correspondence team. This team is responsible for drafting responses to all letters and e-mails to the PM, including invitations, official requests, and all personal correspondence.

The offices of the provincial premiers are set up according to each premier's specific needs. In general they will also include a press secretary, regional political advisers, and policy advisers on the issues that are of greatest importance to the individual province.

The Privy Council Office (PCO)

Many Canadians often hear the term "Privy Council Office" but don't know what it means. Essentially, the

PCO is the most powerful institution in the bureaucracy. In the same way as the prime minister is the central politician to which all other government politicians report, the Privy Council Office is the central bureaucracy to which all other government departments report. As head of the public service, the PCO is responsible for all policy relating to the employment of department officials across government and any issues of public service reform.

The Privy Council Office is the prime minister's department. As such, its role is to provide nonpartisan advice to the prime minister on all policy issues and all government appointments. The PCO is also responsible for preparing the prime minister for meetings with leaders of other countries and major meetings of international organizations.

The PCO's other main role is to act as the cabinet secretariat. It oversees the cabinet agenda and approves all documents to be put before cabinet for consideration. The Privy Council Office also includes a number of other secretariats, including the Secretariat for Intergovernmental Affairs (IGA). IGA has its own minister and manages relations with the governments of the provinces and territories.

The clerk of the Privy Council is the highest ranking official in the central department of government. The clerk is the most powerful bureaucrat in the government and the most senior non-political adviser to the prime minister.

Government Ministers

Ministers are appointed by the prime minister or premier to act as the political head of a government department or agency. All ministers are elected members of Parliament from the governing party. As the elected officials chosen to lead government departments, they are publicly accountable for all decisions and actions taken by a department under their watch.

All ministers essentially have three distinct roles: they are members of cabinet responsible for all departmental matters and representing their departments at the cabinet table; members of Parliament from the governing party who must fulfil all duties to the House of Commons; and M.P.s responsible for all constituency matters and representing their riding to the government. Most ministers will have three different offices to manage these three roles – one in the department, one on Parliament Hill (the "Hill" office), and one in the riding.

Government Departments

Government departments are made up of public servants who do not change with elections. While political ministers rotate with elections or new appointments as a result of a cabinet shuffle, departments provide the stability and continuity of government. To maintain the independence of departments, ministers cannot hire or fire their officials. Public servants operate independently of political events and are hired according to the procedures and requirements of the Public Service Act.

The structure of the government can change, however, and is based on decisions made by cabinet. Cabinet may decide to split a department in two, create a new department, or make any adjustments to the mandate of a department that they desire. Within government, for example, there is an ongoing debate about whether Foreign Affairs and the Canadian International Development Agency (which handles Canadian foreign aid) should be combined into one department or continue to be represented separately at the cabinet table. When departments are combined, there may be a greater tendency to reach a unified position on an issue and greater efficiency in implementing a government policy. On the other hand, maintaining a department's independence can allow it to pursue its mandates more aggressively by giving it a stronger voice at cabinet.[5]

Regardless of how government departments are set up, their primary role is to provide non-partisan, expert advice to the minister on all government decisions. Within a department, the deputy minister is akin to the clerk of the Privy Council in that he or she is the most powerful official at the top of the bureaucratic hierarchy. He or she reports directly to the minister's office and the clerk of the Privy Council. Deputy ministers are responsible for coordinating and managing the work of all divisions or "bureaus"

---

[5] For a brief on how the government is currently structured, see the list of current federal departments and their mandates at www.canada.gc.ca/depts/major/depind_e.html.

of their department. Consequently, they act as a gate-keeper to all information going to the minister's office. The deputy minister is also accountable for all financial decisions of the department and the day-to-day operation of all departmental activities and services.

Whereas ministers tend to take a short-term political view of an issue, deputy ministers can afford to take a long-term view as they are not subject to elections. Although they are required to be politically sensitive in all advice given to ministers, they are expected to remain politically neutral.

HOW PARLIAMENT WORKS[6]

The House of Commons

The House of Commons is Canada's central institution of Parliament. With 232 members representing their ridings across the country, the House is the principal means through which citizens can express their views and participate in decision-making. The daily business of Parliament is incorporated into "Standing Orders" presided over by the Speaker of the House. This daily business includes

- Introducing bills into the legislature.
- "Tabling" documents – or submitting a document to the House so that it will be in the public domain as part of the official record.

---

[6] For more detailed information on the Canadian Parliament, go to www.parl.gc.ca.

- Passing or moving "motions" that express the will of Parliament to the government and to the public.
- Presenting committee reports and committee studies.
- Reading statements by individual members of Parliament.
- Voting on bills in order to pass new legislation or laws.

Each day fifteen minutes is set aside for individual members of Parliament to speak on a particular issue of concern. There are also twenty "Opposition Days" allotted each year for opposition parties to propose motions on any topic they wish to debate. A number of other special debates can be included in the Standing Orders, such as emergency debates on urgent matters and "take-note" debates, which allow members (and ministers) to express their views on an issue without the requirement that a decision be taken.[7]

The Senate

The Senate is the upper chamber of Parliament designed to act as a check and balance to the work of the House of Commons. The Senate was originally created to provide a "sober second thought" to the decisions taken by the House of Commons by the

---

[7] This information is taken from the Compendium, House of Commons Procedures Online posted on the Government of Canada Parliamentary Web site at http://www.parl.gc.ca/compendium/web-content/c_g_typicalsittingday-e.htm#4h.

elected members of Parliament. It was also created to provide some protection for the various regional, provincial, and minority interests in Canada. Its 105 members are appointed by the governor general, on the advice of the prime minister, and they remain members until the age of seventy-five.[8]

In order to become law, a bill must pass through both the House of Commons and the Senate. Like the House, the Senate can amend, delay, or refuse to pass a bill under its consideration. In reality, however, the Senate rarely exercises its power to override the business of the government once the House of Commons has adopted a piece of legislation.

Where the Senate has more influence is through its committee hearings on controversial issues. These committees can choose to conduct special studies on particular topics that cumulate in a report to government containing recommendations that reflect and respond to public opinion. Senate committees, for example, have issued reports on euthanasia and assisted suicide, terrorism, the mass media, Aboriginal veterans, and Canada's retirement policies.

To draft the reports, Senate committees hold public hearings and call in witnesses to provide expert advice. These hearings provide another opportunity for individuals, organizations, and independent experts to get involved. Most committee meetings are held in public, and the committees welcome and

---

[8] The Constitution allows for the appointment of eight additional senators, to a maximum of 113.

receive briefs and requests to appear from all interested Canadians.[9]

In the House of Commons, seats are distributed on the basis of population, but each region of the country is represented by an equal number of seats in the Senate. Additional seats have been added as new provinces and territories were created.

The Role of the Opposition

There are three basic groups of M.P.s: ministers and their parliamentary secretaries; the members who support the government; and the members who oppose the government. The Official Opposition is the opposition party with the largest number of seats in the House. As such, they have certain rights and privileges over and above the other opposition parties. These include the right to ask the first question in Question Period and the right to speak for an unlimited amount of time during specific debates.

Opposition parties work to make sure that differing views on government initiatives are publicly presented and officially expressed. They challenge and debate all proposed government legislation and act as a watchdog on government conduct.

The Leader of the Opposition is usually granted the right to speak first on all government bills and motions immediately after they are introduced by a

---

[9] For more information on how to appear before a Senate Committee, contact the Office of the Principal Clerk at comsen@sen.parl.gc.ca.

government minister. Each opposition party is granted time to debate according to the proportion of seats they have in the House.

Opposition parties sitting on a parliamentary committee have the option of submitting a supplementary or "dissenting" report to Parliament. This "minority report" may include alternative recommendations from members of the opposition that may be presented to the full House following the presentation of the committee's official report.[10]

How a Bill Becomes a Law

1. *Introduction:* A motion is introduced in the House of Commons to put the bill on the parliamentary agenda. Government ministers normally propose the motions for government bills; however, private members can also propose a motion for a private member's bill. Private members' bills are the opposition's main tool to propose a change in policy. A private member's bill can be introduced by any M.P., from any political party on any issue. If the bill has financial implications for the government, however, it requires support from the governing party to pass. While these types of bills rarely go far in a majority government (because they cannot garner the votes in

---

[10] This information is drawn from Maple Leaf Web at http://www.mapleleafweb.com/features/parliament/official-opposition/opposition-days.html.

the House if the government is against them), in a minority government they have a greater chance of passing. A private member's bill must follow all the same procedures as a government bill right through to royal assent.

2. *First Reading:* The content of a new law is introduced to members of Parliament. During this "tabling" phase, there is no debate.

3. *Second Reading:* Debate is held on the bill's principles. Individual members of Parliament are given a chance to speak for or against the major issues raised by the draft legislation. The specific clauses of the bill are not discussed in detail at this stage.

4. *Committee Stage:* Bills that are accepted at second reading move on to the committee stage. To look into the issues more closely, the draft legislation is referred to a subcommittee or standing committee for review. The committee is composed of M.P.s from all parties and is responsible for reading through the bill clause by clause and proposing amendments. At this stage, the committee may hear testimony from outside witnesses to take their views into consideration when proposing amendments to the bill. Once the committee has completed its review, it orders that the bill be reported back to the House of Commons.

5. *Report Stage:* The House reviews the amendments proposed by the committee. It also offers an opportunity for members who did not sit on

the committee to propose their own amendments. All additional amendments may be moved, debated, and voted on at this stage.

6. *Third Reading:* The bill returns to the full House for final reading and debate. A final vote is taken. If some issues are still unresolved, the bill may be referred back to committee for further amendment or reconsideration.

7. *Message to the Senate:* If the majority of members vote in favour, the bill passes and a message is sent to the Senate, requesting that it do the same. At the Senate, the bill will go through the same process as in the House of Commons – first reading, second reading, referral to committee, third reading, and a vote. The key difference is that the Senate can only delay passage or suggest changes to the House, it cannot defeat the bill. There is often another opportunity for public input during Senate committee hearings. Senators may also hear witnesses on controversial issues to help them consider whether additional amendments should be proposed.

8. *Royal Assent:* Once approved by the Senate, the new legislation is sent to the governor general to receive royal assent. A bill must receive royal assent to officially become law.

Note: If the Senate amends a bill, it will be sent back to the House of Commons for a vote on whether the House concurs with the amendments made by the Senate.

Parliamentary Committees

The House of Commons, the Senate, and provincial parliaments have parliamentary committees that convene groups of members of Parliament to study and bring forward recommendations on matters of national importance. Several different types of committees are convened for different reasons, including

- *Committee of the Whole (House)*. All members of the House of Commons sit as a committee (with a chairperson presiding rather than the Speaker of the House) to deliberate on, rather than inquire into, a matter. This will be used for major issues such as the budget, where many M.P.s will want to go on record.
- *Standing Committees*. House of Commons or Senate standing committees are appointed for the term of Parliament to look into specific matters. Standing committees report their findings and make recommendations to the House for consideration. Standing "joint" committees can also be convened to have proportionate numbers of members from both the House and Senate look at an issue.
- *Special Committees*. Special committees are appointed in the House or Senate on an ad hoc basis to investigate special matters. For example, special committees were convened to look into provisions of the Anti-Terrorism Act, the GST (Goods and Services Tax), and the Clean Air Act. A special committee ceases to exist after it has

reported to the House, its deadline expires, or the session of Parliament has come to an end.

- *Legislative Committees.* Legislative committees are appointed to study bills clause by clause. All bills, except those dealing with supply matters, are referred to a legislative committee after second reading.

It should be noted that parliamentary committees are not currently set up to play a major role in exposing maladministration or wrongdoing. As we saw with the sponsorship scandal in 2004, committees have limited powers to investigate or to compel testimony. They are not bound by rules of evidence or procedural fairness.

Beyond issuing reports with recommendations to the government, they also do not play a major role in policy-making. Although much of the discussion on parliamentary reform focuses on strengthening the role of committees (by giving them substantial research budgets, more staff, and more time for sustained questioning) currently, they are structured to focus on holding the government accountable for its actions.

A Note on Provincial Legislatures

Provincial legislatures operate in much the same way as discussed above. The key difference is the absence of a Senate, meaning that once a bill has been passed in its final form by the House, it goes directly to the lieutenant-governor of the province for royal assent.

II. HOW DECISIONS GET MADE

If there is one theme to take away from this book it is this: politicians can't do it alone. Even if you convince the members of Parliament, the ministers, and even the prime minister, elected representatives have surprisingly little power to make changes on their own. If you want to be successful as an advocate, it is absolutely critical that you try to get the bureaucracy onside as much as possible. At the very least, it is important to try to understand where officials are coming from so that you assist in overcoming unwarranted bureaucratic resistance to your ideas.

Here's a real-life example from my experience in a minister's office. During the consultations for the new Immigration and Refugee Protection Act of 2001, there was fierce resistance from powerful officials within the Department of Citizenship and Immigration to the idea of introducing an appeal on the merit of decisions made by the Immigration and Refugee Board. Under the old law, if a mistake was made during the potential life-or-death hearing to decide whether someone was a genuine refugee, the case had to be referred to the courts for a judicial review. During a judicial review, the judge would look only at the question of whether all appropriate procedures were followed, and not at the substance of the decision – whether the person's testimony was credible and whether they were genuinely at risk.[11] If

---

[11] A person is considered to be genuinely at risk if they are found to have a well-founded fear of persecution based on race, religion, nationality, political opinion, or membership in a particular social group.

the courts determined that there was procedural error, the case would be sent back to the Immigration and Refugee Board to be heard all over again.

Advocates argued that a judicial review was inadequate. Following the lead of other like-minded countries around the world, they maintained that Canada should include the opportunity to appeal the merit of the decision itself. The serious consequences of sending someone back to a country where they could face persecution, torture, or death requires a second look at the substantive issues.

Officials in the Department of Citizenship and Immigration argued that introducing an appeal would simply add another step that would keep failed refugee claimants in Canada longer. Lawyers working within the system countered that introducing a paper appeal on the merit of the decision would actually be faster and more fair because there would be a way to correct errors in the first instance and avoid going through the lengthy process of judicial review in the courts. Even in cases where the person was deemed to be a security risk, advocates maintained that in a globalized world, removing terrorists to countries with less-developed judicial and law-enforcement capacity than our own would not isolate Canada from the problem nor make us safer.

This issue became a major focal point in the debate around the new law. In the end, the minister was convinced that introducing an appeal on the merit of the decision was the right thing to do. Provisions to set up a new appeal division within the

Immigration and Refugee Board were incorporated into a draft government bill. The bill was approved by cabinet and introduced into the House of Commons for parliamentary review. During both House and Senate committee hearings, the three "wise men" of the department (as they were called by some officials) testified before committee as to why they thought introducing an appeal was a bad idea. In both the House and the Senate, the arguments of the officials were rejected in favour of those made by advocates, and the bill passed both Houses and received royal assent in early 2002.

Despite the fact that advocates convinced politicians, the cabinet, the House, and the Senate, the appeal still does not exist today. What happened? Once the bill became law, it fell back to those same officials to take the next steps to implement the new policy. Through creative bureaucratic manoeuvring, the funding for the new appeal process was separated from the funding to implement the rest of the bill. The new law was implemented and is still in force today, with the exception of the new Refugee Appeal Division.

When a department is fiercely opposed to a decision by its minister, there are innumerable ways it can delay, misinterpret, or avoid following through on the instructions by elected decision-makers. For example, if subsequent ministers fail to request that the funding for the new Refugee Appeal Division (RAD) come forward or the department just fails to point out that this request needs to be made, officials can simply wait out the term of an unpopular minister (or government) until the time is politically right to revisit a decision that they disagree with.

Although the example is extreme, the main point is valid: advocates for any cause must work with both the politicians *and* the bureaucracy to see their "win" translated into government policy. For any advocacy campaign to be successful, it is imperative to develop an awareness and respect for bureaucratic processes so that your strategy acknowledges the hugely important role officials play in the outcome of any policy decision.

THE POLICY PROCESS

Policy refers to any course of action adopted and pursued by a government.[12] In general, there are four stages to the policy process.[13]

1. Setting the Agenda

The elected government in power sets out an agenda based on promises made during the election. Before the election, political parties gather ideas from any number of sources. These can include party research bureaus, key constituency groups, academic think-tanks, the media, polling firms, and for-profit and

---

[12] *Dictionary.com Unabridged (v 1.0.1)*. Based on the Random House Unabridged Dictionary, © Random House, Inc. 2006. 25 Nov. 2006, Dictionary.com http://dictionary.reference.com/browse/policy.

[13] YMCA Manual and Toolkit, *Be H.I.P.P: Have Influence on Public Policy*, sets out a good basic framework to understand government decision-making.

not-for-profit organizations. Once elected, political leaders will then consult with the central bureaucracies of the government to see what is feasible from the official's point of view. The central agencies include the Privy Council Office, the Finance Department, and the Treasury Board. Together, the officials and government ministers, led by the prime minister, will work on drafting the Speech from the Throne. Once the Speech from the Throne is read, political commitments are repeated and explained in more detail through ministerial speeches, political announcements, caucus groups, and departmental Web sites.[14]

2. Policy Design

How a policy will actually work is mostly driven by the bureaucracy. The Speech from the Throne essentially directs government departments to begin work on implementation. Because elected politicians cannot possibly evaluate all the possible implications of implementing a proposed policy on their own, government departments with expertise on the various issues take the lead on policy design. At this stage, politicians do not usually get involved in the details. Their role can range from ensuring that the bureaucracies provide opportunities for public consultation and that various groups are treated fairly to

---

[14] The Speech from the Throne in discussed in further detail in Chapter 2 on Building Credibility. For more information on the Finance Department and Treasury Board see Chapter 5 on the Budget Cycle.

trying to minimize or block opportunities for public input on issues they expect to be controversial. Generally, however, discussion papers are issued, formal and informal consultations may be set up, and special citizen advisory committees or task forces may be convened. Meanwhile, departments will evaluate the new political commitments to determine how much they will cost, where the money will come from, and whether existing commitments should be altered or sustained. They will also assess the new commitments to determine whether new legislation is needed to implement a policy or existing legislation needs to be amended. Once the policy design is complete, it is sent to the relevant minister for final sign-off. The minister's office will take a political lens to the issue. The minister will decide whether the policy will be well received politically and whether changes need to be made to accommodate various concerns.

3. Cabinet Review

At cabinet, ministers evaluate the final design of the policy and make a political decision about whether to go ahead, how much money to allocate, and when to launch the new initiative. They will discuss whether the final policy lives up to their political commitments and what the public reaction will be. Ministers will also discuss how the policy will be perceived in the media, who is likely to speak publicly as a main opponent, and the causes for any negative public reaction.

4. Legislative Approval

As discussed earlier in this chapter, if a policy requires legislative change, it will go through both houses of Parliament for approval. At this stage, changes to the policy are made only through amendments.

WHO IS THE ACTUAL DECISION-MAKER?

This is a straightforward question but the answer can be very confusing because there are a number of places where the final decision can rest. A decision can be taken at many levels of the bureaucracy and there is a great deal of ministerial authority delegated to officials in a minister's department. At the Canadian Customs and Revenue Agency, for example, the authority to decide what you can and cannot bring into Canada is delegated all the way down to the individual customs officer you meet at the airport. Of

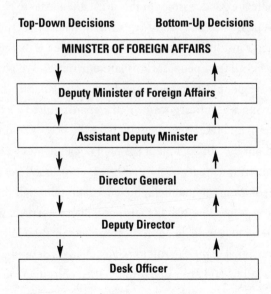

125

course, that officer makes her decision based on the laws, regulations, and guidelines set out for her by the department. Nonetheless, through delegated ministerial authority, she has the power to make a specific decision on your case.

What you need to know, therefore, is how to determine the level of delegation for your particular decision. To simplify what this means for you, there are generally two ways that decisions get made in government.

Bottom-Up Decisions

One of the curious features of our system is that ministers are not usually appointed for their expertise in a given portfolio. A banker can become minister of National Defence and a working mum minister of Citizenship and Immigration. Despite the politics, there are good reasons for this. First, the idea is to give average citizens control over the bureaucracies and major institutions of the country. The idea is that we elect ordinary people who share our values. We give these people the best expert advice available (by having an entire government department to serve them) and then trust them to make the best decisions on our behalf. Second, if the pool of candidates were limited to experts in the field, you could soon get a small group of qualified elite circulating through the same roles. The risk is that these elite, as experts in one area, could become entrenched in their own views, making it difficult to reflect changes desired by the public and expressed through their constituencies.

The downside is that you can get someone with no experience suddenly in charge of a host of issues they know nothing about. They can be required to quickly make highly technical decisions that have huge ramifications nation-wide. Even if they were an expert in their field, ministers cannot possibly have the time to thoroughly research the dozens of important decisions that need to be made on a daily basis. As a result, the majority of decisions that come across ministers' desks are largely run by departments. Ministers rely on the expertise and experience of their departments to research and analyze each issue, present options, and make recommendations. A minister will often choose a handful of issues to follow closely but the vast majority of everyday decisions in a minister's office are made "bottom up." This means a policy direction or action is suggested by the lower levels of the department. It then goes through all appropriate levels of a department hierarchy, gets cross-checked by all internal mechanisms of consultation, and is then presented in a formal memo to the minister for sign-off.

Let's look at a typical bottom-up decision as an example. This example is for a federal department, but provincial departments work in much the same way. A desk officer working at Foreign Affairs may be following events unfolding in Zimbabwe. There may be recent reports of journalists subdued, critics silenced, and the opposition parties obstructed from participating in politics in a meaningful way. The desk officer will have some initial discussions with her boss, the deputy director of Eastern and Southern Africa, and the staff working at our embassy in the region, and they may come to the conclusion that Canada should send an official *"démarche"* to the Mugabe government expressing our concern at a specific action the government took, or failed to take. A *démarche* is an official communiqué expressing a message from one government to another. The *démarche* could be sent through official channels or delivered in person by our ambassador. If the issue is likely to be politically sensitive, the ambassador would need to go through all the appropriate levels of the department for approval. A typical chain of command for this type of decision in the Department of Foreign Affairs would be as follows.

"Don't discount lower-level officials. They can be your best opportunity for input if they are the one holding the pen."
Dominique Raynauld, CIDA (Canadian International Development Agency) Official

The desk officer for Zimbabwe would draft the initial memo that would be sent up to the deputy director for input and approval. Once satisfied, the deputy director would pass the amended memo to the director general (DG) of the Africa Bureau. The DG would weigh the request for a *démarche* in Zimbabwe against other events happening in the region to determine whether a *démarche* on this particular issue makes sense at the time. If the answer is yes, the DG would present the memo to the assistant deputy minister (ADM) for Bilateral Relations with a recommendation that a *démarche* is a priority for the Africa Bureau. The ADM, depending on the level of sensitivity, may or may not amend the memo before sending it up to the deputy minister for approval. The deputy minister's office then acts as gatekeeper to all the memos, from all bureaus, going to the minister's office on a given day. The DM's office would then decide whether to send the memo back down for revision, amend it themselves, or pass it up to the minister's office at the appropriate time.

Of course, if the issue is urgent, a few or many of these steps could be bypassed or happen very quickly. A series of phone calls could refine the language of the *démarche* and the changes to the memo could happen after the fact. Regardless of its urgency, this is the process that officials working in the department feel obligated to respect. Going over their head is never a good idea. While things may move faster, the consequences will surely catch up later on another issue.

In other cases, ministerial authority to make the decision itself may be delegated downward to an operational officer. This means that regular government officials are authorized to make decisions on behalf of the minister, without going through all the usual channels of authority. An example of this is immigration officers, who use delegated ministerial authority to make decisions on whether or not someone is allowed into Canada every day. In these circumstances, legislation, regulation, and policy directives set the parameters for the individual officer's decisions. By law, every decision made by a government official on the minister's behalf is subject to judicial review by the court. This means that when decision-making authority is delegated downwards there are one or more opportunities for appeal or review.

Whether a memo needs to go all the way up to the minister's office for approval depends on how politically sensitive the issue is. If the issue is not likely to garner much public or media attention, final authority to make the decision may rest at any level along the way. The best way to find out who is responsible for making the decision on your particular issue is to ask. Generally the rule is that if the decision is considered "routine," it is delegated. Yet if there are public concerns raised about a delegated authority, it can be bumped up to the political level at any time.

Top-Down Decisions

Of course, decisions can also be made from the top down. This occurs when the prime minister or a minister of a particular department initiates a policy shift and then asks the department to carry it out.

In my experience, this is not as common as you think. There are areas where ministers have enormous power, and others in which they have very little. As the case of the fight for a Refugee Appeal Division illustrates, one of the surprising things about Ottawa is how little power ministers actually have to take a decision on their own if there is significant resistance to that decision in their bureaucracy. A decision taken unilaterally by a minister is rarely sustainable because the bureaucracy will be slow to implement it, or it can be dragged out indefinitely and never be implemented at all. If, however, the minister manages to get enough political support to show that the government as a whole is serious about implementing the policy *and* there are pockets of the bureaucracy willing to support the work, top-down decisions can happen.

WHO INFLUENCES THE DECISION?

Now that we've looked at the basic way a decision can be made, let's look at where the advice to government is coming from. There are many sources of influence on a government decision. The list includes other divisions within a department, other departments, the Privy Council office, the Prime Minister's or Premier's Office, caucus, opposition parties, corporate lobby groups, non-governmental organizations, church groups, coalitions, wide-spread public campaigns, and individuals making powerful arguments at the right time and place. Decisions may also be influenced by other levels of government (federal, provincial, municipal) and international organizations.

Internal Government Consultations

Government is currently organized into separate departments where each hierarchy is more or less responsible for a distinct set of issues. In the past, organizing the government into separate silos made sense. When an urgent decision needed to be taken to protect the public's health, for example, it would go up through the hierarchy of the Health Department to be made by the minister of Health, in consultation with the cabinet. Advocates wanting to have an impact on that decision would focus on getting the officials and minister of one department on the same page.

As the issues become more multi-dimensional, the lines between various government departments are increasingly blurred. Almost every federal department (and many provincial ones as well) is involved in one form or another in international relations. While the Department of Foreign Affairs is still the home of diplomats, officials from other government departments are negotiating international treaties on everything from agricultural issues to international declarations on cultural diversity.

For advocates this means that even if a minister wants to take the lead on an issue that cuts across departmental lines, he or she not only has to work through one department, but will almost certainly have to back up and wait for the issue to work its way up through several other departmental hierarchies as well. The bottom line is that for many issues today advocates have to focus on not just one but several government departments and how they interact.

Top-down and bottom-up decisions require consultation between the silos to ensure that they have enough internal support. Consultations between bureaus of a department are called *intra-departmental* consultations.[15] Formal discussions that take place between departments are called *inter-departmental*

---

[15] Some departments refer to their various sections as "bureaus," and others use words like "divisions" to reflect the same concept.

consultations. Depending on the issue, there may also be formal consultations with the provinces and/or the municipalities.

By looking at a list of government departments, you can make an educated guess as to which departments will be consulted on your issue. For example, if your issue concerns the avian flu, it is reasonable to assume that Health Canada, Agriculture Canada, and Foreign Affairs may all be consulted. Within each department, organizational charts can give you an idea of which specific bureaus will be involved.[16] Within Health Canada, it is likely that the Health Policy Branch (which deals with intergovernmental and international affairs) and the Public Health Agency of Canada (which is responsible for responding to public health emergencies and infectious disease outbreaks) would both have a role.

Aside from looking at who is likely to be consulted on your issue, it is also important to look at who is *not* consulted. Sometimes a critical goal for advocacy is to make sure that the right bureau of a department is brought into a discussion in order to make sure that a certain perspective is on the table. One of the major challenges I faced at Foreign Affairs was how to help integrate the perspectives of the Human Rights and Human Security Bureaus into the broader decisions of the department on questions of international security and trade.

---

[16] Locating departmental organizational charts is discussed in detail in Chapter 9, "Who Do You Need to Know?"

THE ART OF THE POSSIBLE

How Does a Decision Get to Cabinet?

If an issue is controversial or could have a significant impact on other aspects of the government, a minister will need to present it to cabinet for a decision.

Here's how these types of decisions work:

- Before any issue is brought to cabinet, it must go through both intra-departmental consultations and inter-departmental consultations. During both of these processes, others within government have a chance to raise objections and present opposing points of view.
- Lead departments then prepare memorandums to cabinet, or MCs for short. MCs are large documents that give the background and rationale for the major issues the government needs to take a decision on. Each MC will offer recommendations on how the government can move forward along with options on how the initiative could be funded.
- Once all levels of the bureaucratic hierarchy have signed off, the MC is passed up to the political level for approval. The minister's office of the lead department must give its sanction to the final document and ministers must be prepared to formally present it to cabinet for a decision.

It is up to the lead department to decide what makes it into the final draft of their MC and how an issue is presented. The Privy Council Office (PCO), however, acts as the ultimate gatekeeper of the cabinet agenda and determines which MCs are ready to be brought to cabinet for decision. It can therefore ask departments to make changes to accommodate either its own views or the views of other departments. If, even after inter-departmental consultations, one department persists in having serious concerns about an aspect of another department's MC, the PCO may delay putting the item on the cabinet agenda. In cases where urgency requires that the controversial issue be brought for a decision despite concerns raised by another depart-ment, the minister of the dissenting department will be briefed by his or her officials to raise their depart-ment's concerns at the cabinet table.

At cabinet, ministers make a political calculation on how to move forward. They will weigh the con-cerns raised by various departments against a number of political factors. Will the people who like the policy be vocal with their support or will they just say it doesn't go far enough? Do the bureaucratic con-cerns outweigh the political ones? Is it worth delaying a decision until concerns can be addressed or is it more urgent to act now?

Ultimately, the ministers will make a political decision whether to go ahead with the existing MC, delay approval, and ask that changes be made or deny approval altogether.

HOW IS A DECISION IMPLEMENTED?

Once a cabinet decision is made, the implementa-tion of a decision may fall to any number of depart-ments. Generally, memorandums to cabinet lay out the specific responsibilities of each department in implementing a policy decision. They also state how the money will be divided up between departments to fund various programs and expenses. For example, Health Canada, Citizenship and Immigration, and the Department of Heritage may all have a role to play in implementing a specific policy. Health Canada may be required to pay for part of the initiative from a source of funds within the department's existing budget. The Department of Canadian Heritage may have to change a law or regulation under its jurisdiction. Citizenship and Immigration may be asked to add a factor for consideration in making decisions on specific cases. All departments may have to issue new internal documents to inform employees of the changes and reinforce the new rules through training.

In reality, if inter-departmental consultations fail to resolve these detailed questions before the cabinet decision is made, implementation of the decision can be delayed indefinitely. This is where we get empty announcements that don't translate into action. Because it is impossible to anticipate all the detailed discussions necessary to implement a proposed policy, the longer a government is in power, the more reluctant ministers can become to make promises without thoroughly checking with all bureaucratic channels.

Clearly, advocating at the political level is not enough. For an advocacy strategy to be successful, you have to work both top down and bottom up. This means developing contacts at both levels and working to get alternative sources of information into the documents prepared by departments and into the hands at the minister's office directly. Keep in mind that it is the bureaucracy that will be implementing any policy decision. If you garner the support of officials early on, it is more likely that a policy decision will be implemented in a way that is sustainable.

CHAPTER FIVE

HOW DOES THE MONEY FLOW?

The Budget Cycle

Now that we've looked at common obstacles to getting a proposal through the bureaucracy, we turn to the issue of funding. Although this book is not about how to lobby for money, it will look at how money flows through the government. Understanding this process is important because being able to identify a source of funding for a policy change can be the biggest obstacle you face. Even if a new policy is already funded, it can be a great help to understand the budget cycle and the roles of the Finance Department and the Treasury Board. Groups and individuals that know how the budget cycle works are more likely to be met with a positive reception because they have taken into account a major bureaucratic constraint. To this end, the chapter will show you how a department goes about releasing government funds. The chapter concludes with some strategies on how to position your issue vis-à-vis the budget cycle so that it has the best chance of success.

Of course government funding does not always follow a clear and logical path. As we all know, there are many instances where corners are cut and funds may be released quickly by bypassing the usual channels. While these are the stories that make the news, the reality is that the vast majority of proposals do go through the formal government process, with all of its checks and balances, before any money is released. Although it may be tempting to try to tap into the fast track, experience shows that decisions made outside the formal process are rarely sustainable. A group may get one-time funding for a specific event, but they usually find they have damaged their reputation, irritated important people they may need to work with in the future, and hurt their credibility for the next time they approach government with a legitimate cause.

WHY CAN'T POLITICIANS KEEP THEIR PROMISES?

Once a year (usually late winter or early spring), with a lot of media fanfare, the prime minister or premier makes a big public announcement about the government's budget. Pundits from all sides debate the merits of the different commitments while the government launches a massive communications campaign to defend its choices. Groups and individuals across the country get excited when they hear that millions of dollars have been earmarked for a program or policy they have been pushing for over time. Then suddenly, nothing happens. It seems as though weeks and months go by and these programs are still nowhere to be seen. Why does this happen? With all those tax dollars at its disposal, why can't the government seem to write a simple cheque?

Bureaucratic Checks and Balances

The formal budget announcement is made only after cabinet approves the government's financial intentions for the year. If a proposal makes it into the budget, however, it does not mean that the item is guaranteed to be funded. A government department still has to present a detailed business plan to justify exactly how it plans to spend the money. Federally, departments present this in the form of a submission to the Treasury Board (TB). The TB is responsible for making sure that departmental business plans meet the standards and regulations set by the government to sanction the use of taxpayer's money. Provincially, a similar institution – the Management Board of Ontario, for instance – fulfils a parallel function for the provincial budget.

The Treasury Board considers how much money is needed and whether requests for funding will adhere to the targets set out in the budget. They will ask questions such as: What exactly are you going to do with this money? How are you going to justify each dollar that is spent? Is this a one-time expenditure or will it be ongoing over several years? They look at how a department plans to monitor the spending of this money and how it will evaluate whether it has met its objectives. All departments need the Treasury to approve their submission before any proposal can go forward. If the board has problems with a departmental submission, all programs and policy initiatives will be delayed until the problem is worked out.

For advocates, this may be the cause of some confused messages or meetings. While waiting for Treasury Board approval, officials will be cautious or even evasive to avoid raising expectations before they know they have the money to go ahead. The omnibus bills that outline general government expenditures to Parliament are available to the public, but the Treasury Board submissions are formal documents from ministers to a "central agency" and, as such, are not available for public release.

Once the Treasury approves departmental submissions, it presents them to Parliament for review. Parliament is then asked to approve all federal department spending plans by passing two omnibus bills under the Appropriations Act. The "Main Estimates" is a comprehensive bill outlining who has spending authority and how much money is set to be spent. The "Supplementary Estimates" are passed later in the year to make adjustments or corrections to the Main Estimates as required.

To address the lag between the budget announcement and the formal approval of the estimates by Parliament, the governor general has the power to keep the government running by passing an interim supply bill. The Interim Supply Bill is a bill to give a portion of the funds to departments in advance of

Parliament passing the estimates so that departments can start to spend the money in the spring, before it is reimbursed to them in the fall.

In a majority government, votes on the estimates are routine housekeeping measures that are usually passed easily. In a minority government, however, theses votes can become critical as they can represent a vote of confidence in the government in power. We saw this clearly when Paul Martin's minority government was forced to make concessions to the NDP (New Democratic Party) to pass the budget of 2005. But a minority government can also present another challenge: departments may not be as willing to spend money announced in the February budget on faith that the estimates will be passed by Parliament in the fall. Therefore, an initiative announced in February may not see its money flow for some time. This can cause any number of delays in implementing the commitments that were already announced to the public.

Political Checks and Balances

While the Treasury and Management Boards control the bureaucratic spending of the money, the minister of Finance and the Finance Department oversee the political decisions on who gets how much and why.

Political decisions to fund major policy proposals are made in one of two ways. At an opportune time for the government, the full cabinet meets to conduct a strategy session to assess the results of the last budget and identify the big priorities for the new budget.

Additionally, cabinet committees made up of a subset of ministers from various departments meet to look at decisions on a specific set of shared files. Cabinet committees on economic affairs, social affairs, foreign affairs, or national security, for instance, are made up of a select group of ministers who oversee the specific design and implementation of policies approved in the last budget. They are also responsible for responding to direction from full cabinet on which new policy proposals to articulate and bring to fruition.

When a proposal goes through cabinet, it is approved as either a "funded" or "unfunded" Memorandum to Cabinet (MC). Funded MCs are those for which a source of funds has already been identified. Every year, all unfunded MCs get fed into a political priority-setting exercise that involves further consultation between ministers, the minister of Finance, and the prime minister. To assist with the political decisions, the Department of Finance will ask questions such as "What will you use this money for? Why should this initiative take precedence over other government priorities?"

Essentially, the Finance Department oversees the big picture. The Finance minister and his or her department have the political task of making sure the money is spent on government priorities in a manner that allows the government to meet its political commitments. This means setting the fiscal framework, managing the debt, and overseeing tax and fiscal policy, and the macroeconomic outlook for the country as a whole.

THE BUDGET CYCLE

To get a better idea of what the system looks like as a whole, the following graph shows key events in the budget cycle over the course of one year.[1] Notice that planning for year two is well underway before the estimates are passed, finally distributing the funds from year one. This point is important because it will show you why there is a lag between when money is announced and when the cheque can actually be written.

In general the appropriations bills – or the spending authority for the government – consists of

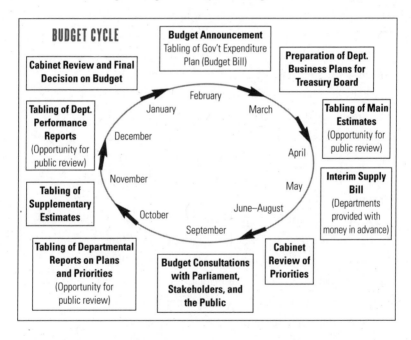

---

[1] The graph was developed from a Treasury Board briefing note entitled "The Expenditure Management System of the Government of Canada, Feb 1995."

three parts. The Government Expenditure Plan provides an overview of government spending. The
Main Estimates identify who can spend the money
and how much they can spend. The Departmental
Expenditure Plans, which include both department
reports on plans and priorities and departmental
performance reports, lay out the specific authorities
of each department. It is important to note that all
bills must be passed through both the House of
Commons and the Senate. After receiving Senate
approval, they go to the governor general to receive
royal assent.

To take a look at what's happening in more detail,
below is a month-by-month breakdown of events. Of
course, the exact dates for certain events vary each
year, but the above graph gives you a basic picture of
what you can expect and when. Although it can be a
lot to absorb, stick with it because understanding how
the budget works can be the single factor in helping
you succeed with your cause. At a minimum, it will
help you understand where officials are coming from
when responding to your request.

February
- The minister of Finance delivers the Budget
  Speech and announces the government's budget-
  ary priorities for the year.

March
- Departments and agencies across government
  prepare detailed business plans for submission to
  the Treasury Board.

- The Main Estimates are usually tabled in Parliament close to the budget announcement on or before March 1. In the House of Commons, the Main Estimates are then reviewed by the appropriate standing committee of M.P.s and there are opportunities for public input or review. This usually occurs sometime between March and June.

April

- The Interim Supply Bill is introduced.

June–August

- Cabinet committees, ministers, and the Privy Council Office start to develop the cabinet priorities for the following year.
- At the bureaucratic level, departments start to integrate the advice from cabinet committees, the Treasury Board, and parliamentary standing committees to develop options that will be presented to the Finance minister for the next budget (year 2).

September/October

- The minister of Finance and the Finance Department release budget consultation papers. The House Standing Committee on Finance, stakeholders, and the general public have an opportunity to review and comment on the government's proposals.
- The committee will submit a final report on the fiscal strategy for the upcoming budget (year 2). Central agencies (the Privy Council Office, the Department of Finance, and Treasury Board)

will gather feedback from these consultations and prepare options for ministers to consider at cabinet.

October/November
- Departments table a Report on Plans and Priorities, which are individual expenditure plans for the next one to three years. These include more specific statements on how each bureau within a department plans to spend its money.

Late November
- Supplementary Estimates are tabled. These make adjustments to the Main Estimates as required.
- Departmental performance reports – which discuss whether departments have met targets and performance expectations from the previous fiscal year – are also tabled.
- Meanwhile, the minister of Finance will develop the budget strategy for year 2, drawing on the feedback from the consultation papers, the recommendations from the Standing Committee on Finance, the recommendations of cabinet policy committees, and the options put forward by the Treasury Board.

December/January
- Cabinet reviews the budget strategy for year 2. The prime minister and the minister of Finance make the final spending decisions.

So where do you fit in? Throughout the cycle, "stakeholders," or those with a particular interest in a specific cause, are invited, along with the public, to participate in a number of ways. First, you can provide comments to individual ministers, specific departments, or the minister of Finance by sending in a written brief. Second, you can participate in any formal consultation process organized by the government. Third, some stakeholders are invited to comment on proposed spending plans by testifying before parliamentary standing committees set up to look at the issues. Various House standing committees review and report on the Main Estimates and on the individual departmental outlooks and performance reports. This process offers an opportunity to review departmental budgets line by line and ask questions or offer recommendations. The Standing Committee on Finance, for instance, reviews and reports on the budget consultation papers. It also makes formal recommendations to the government on amendments to the proposed budget strategy.

HOW A DEPARTMENT TAKES A PROPOSAL THROUGH THE BUDGET CYCLE

It is also useful to look at the budget cycle from the other perspective – that of an official trying to take a policy proposal through the system. This will help give you a sense of the language officials use when talking about the status of an initiative and the specific challenges they face when trying to get the funds for a project that has been approved.

Take one official's experience as an example. A Treasury Board submission was written in July for an item that had been announced as part of the budget

HOW A DEPARTMENT TAKES A PROPOSAL THROUGH THE BUDGET

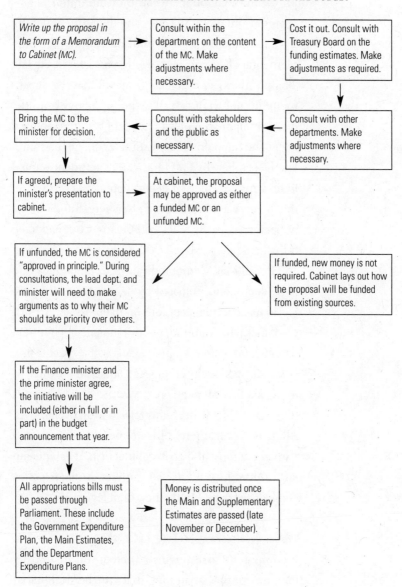

Write up the proposal in the form of a Memorandum to Cabinet (MC). →

Consult within the department on the content of the MC. Make adjustments where necessary. →

Cost it out. Consult with Treasury Board on the funding estimates. Make adjustments as required.

↓

Consult with other departments. Make adjustments where necessary. ←

Consult with stakeholders and the public as necessary. ←

Bring the MC to the minister for decision.

↓

If agreed, prepare the minister's presentation to cabinet. →

At cabinet, the proposal may be approved as either a funded MC or an unfunded MC.

↙ ↘

If unfunded, the MC is considered "approved in principle." During consultations, the lead dept. and minister will need to make arguments as to why their MC should take priority over others.

If funded, new money is not required. Cabinet lays out how the proposal will be funded from existing sources.

↓

If the Finance minister and the prime minister agree, the initiative will be included (either in full or in part) in the budget announcement that year.

↓

All appropriations bills must be passed through Parliament. These include the Government Expenditure Plan, the Main Estimates, and the Department Expenditure Plans. →

Money is distributed once the Main and Supplementary Estimates are passed (late November or December).

the previous February. Treasury Board gave its approval in September. Because of the minority government situation, however, the department did not want to spend the money until it knew that the Supplementary Estimates Bill would pass later in the fall. The possibility of an election meant that the department did not want to risk spending money from the Interim Supply Bill now in hopes of being reimbursed later. The Supplementary Estimates did not pass until late December. By that time, the department wanted to do a further internal departmental review to see if the money was more needed elsewhere. Funds for the project were finally received January 15 but had to be fully spent before March 31, the end of that fiscal year.

Recall that Memorandums to Cabinet (MCs) are large documents prepared by departments for ministers to make formal decisions on major issues. All MCs contain the background, policy rationale, recommendations, and options for proceeding with a specific proposal. An MC usually embraces a larger theme, such as the Canadian Strategy on HIV/AIDS, which covers a number of specific decisions related to an overall goal. All new government bills to be introduced into Parliament must also go to cabinet first. At cabinet, an MC to introduce a bill will outline all major policy changes contained in the new draft legislation.

How Can Understanding the Budget Help You?

It is important to distinguish whether you are looking for new money or money that can be designated from an existing source. If a source of funds can be identified, your task is to persuade those in charge of managing the fund that your project fits with the government's objectives and represents the best use of the taxpayer's money to accomplish a common goal. If a source of funds cannot be identified but your proposal is approved in principle, it will be included in a request for new money and entered into the priority-setting process. Here your task is to assist officials in making arguments as to why this issue should be a priority.

STRATEGIES TO FIND FUNDING

STEP 1: Try to Identify an Existing Source of Funds

Money can flow more quickly if your proposal fits within an existing departmental budget. The Web sites of the various departments usually contain a fairly comprehensive list of the programs a department is currently running. The goal here is to look for an existing budget that can accommodate your proposal. To look a little closer, examine the department's annual Report on Plans and Priorities. These reports are available either on the parliamentary Web site at www.parl.gc.ca or on the Web site of the department itself. They will give you a sense of how different bureaus within a department spend their money and should help you identify the specific bureau that is responsible for the most appropriate budget. With that information in hand, you can use departmental organizational charts to identify the key officials in a bureau who manage that particular budget.

> "On funding requests, don't go about it wrong. 'If you don't give me more money, we'll go under' just doesn't work."
> Treasury Board Official

151

If a source of funds cannot be identified, your strategy should focus on helping the relevant department make its case to the Finance Department and the prime minister's office. Here the goal is to identify the specific department, bureaus, and officials who will be bringing your issue for decision. Help them articulate the cost of not taking action now and develop the arguments as to why this issue should be a priority above others. At times they may even need your help to overcome internal opposition but may be uncomfortable asking for it.

> **"Start from where they are, not from where you are."**
> Paul Genest, Former Senior Adviser to Prime Minister Jean Chrétien

STEP 2: Prepare Your Case

The Reports on Plans and Priorities can give you a general sense of how much your proposal would change the way the money is currently spent. Take a look at how much money is spent on each of the department's designated priorities. Will your proposal require 20 per cent or 80 per cent of the existing budget? The level of resistance you will face will vary with the amount of change that is required. A proposal that is consistent with the stated purpose of an existing program will have a much better chance of success than one that asks a department to fundamentally change its priorities.

It is also a good idea to pay particular attention to the department's stated objectives for how that money should be spent. Frame your proposal in a way that uses the government's language and fits within its objectives. Argue why you think there is a better way to spend this money. Also remember that monies approved for existing programs may have to be spent by the end of the fiscal year, March 31. This means that by January or February of that year, departments may be looking for justifiable ways to spend unused funds.

STEP 3: Target the Bureaucracy First

If a source of funds can be identified, your efforts should always be directed at the level of officials first.[2] Listen carefully to any obstacles raised by officials during initial discussions. They will give you a sense of the internal challenges officials are facing in bringing a proposal forward. Jumping to politicians too early can alienate those who manage the funds every day and cause undue resistance within a department. Focus on building support both inside and outside of the lead department. Demonstrate to officials how your organization can best use these resources to achieve your shared objectives.

It is a myth that ministers can simply bypass the system and write a cheque directly. Although ministers may have some discretionary funding attached to their offices, it is generally not enough to fund and sustain a policy initiative. Even if the minister had the funds directly, politicians know that all their budgets are available to the public through the Access to

---

[2] Efforts may include attending meetings, writing letters, making phone calls, or organizing events. For more on how to choose your tactics and run effective meetings, see Chapters 10, 11, and 12.

Information Act and therefore they have to exercise some degree of caution.[3]

The vast majority of funding decisions, therefore, go through the entire bureaucratic review process before being brought to a minister for final approval. This includes memos on funding decisions to renew, expand, or cut programs and proposals to create new ones. It also includes everything from travel expenses to organizing events and setting up public consultations. Once a funding memo is presented to the minister, it is very difficult to override a decision of their department, even if they want to. In addition to the risk of negative press, ministers want assurance and backup for the funding decisions they make. If a proposal has not yet been through the department, a minister will request that a department first evaluate a proposal that they find interesting.

> "You need to make the case you are the best thing around town. Here's what a good job we're doing and here's why we are a good investment."
>
> Official, Treasury Board

> "Always remember that politicians are trying to balance competing interests."
>
> Anita Neville, M.P., Winnipeg South Centre

STEP 4: Pay Attention to Timing and Work with the Budget Cycle

It is always important to tie your issue to the current government agenda. Many issues are funded in three- to five-year increments. If your program is funded only every five years, there is no sense making arguments to change the funding structure at year 3. Within the funding period, it may be possible to make

---

[3] Through the Access to Information Act, ministerial spending, departmental spending, and even internal briefing notes can all be accessed for public scrutiny. With the exception of matters deemed to be important for national security, the government is under a legal obligation to release as much information as possible. The definition of national security has recently been called into question through the Maher Arar case.

minor adjustments to how funds are allocated. For any major changes in how the money is spent, however, it may be necessary to wait until the entire strategy on the issue comes up for renewal.

STEP 5: Bring in the Politicians and Help Them Make Their Case

As a last resort, bring in people at the political level. Offer to speak to a caucus committee that has expressed an interest in your issue. Help interested M.P.s make the case to the lead minister. Approach the minister or the minister's office directly to see if there are opportunities to make your views known.

In all cases, make sure you have a sense of what other issues are competing for the government's attention and why your particular issue should be a priority. It is also important to be aware of what the bureaucratic concerns are and where they are coming from. Unless you can provide good evidence and convincing responses to concerns in advance, ministers will most likely share their department's hesitancy.

Once again, in presenting your case to politicians, always highlight how your proposal fits with stated government priorities. Look at the issue from the politicians' point of view so that you can make the strongest arguments that resonate with them.

While following these steps may seem difficult and quite involved, it is worth it. Simply paying attention to the budget cycle over the course of one session of Parliament will make you familiar enough with the key points to be much more effective as an advocate. Whatever your cause, this information will greatly

"Post-tsunami, a relief group called a large meeting with officials, who thought that it was going to be a request for money. Instead, the group said, 'Here is our experience in post-disaster situations. Here's what we have learned. Here's some mistakes we often see.' Officials were blown away. The group ended the meeting by asking, 'What can we do for you?' Officials scrambled to take notes and wanted to look for ways to fund them."
Official, Canadian International Development Agency

strengthen your case and magnify the impact of your actions. Don't get discouraged if your issue isn't funded quickly. There are good reasons that money takes time to flow. In fact, as we all know, if the money flows too quickly there is usually cause for concern. The best strategy is to identify your window and make the strongest arguments for how the taxpayer's money can best be spent.

CHAPTER SIX

WHEN IS A GOOD TIME?

Creating a Timeline

Timing is everything. No matter how good your recommendations are they have got to be presented at the right time in order to have an impact on government policy. We all do things at the last minute, but if you really want to be effective it is important to learn to read the signs for good timing. The right time for your issue will depend on who the actual decision-maker is, who influences the decision, and when those you are talking to have it within their power to make it happen.

For a ministerial decision, the right time may be just before a cabinet meeting in advance of an international event. For an M.P., it may be just as a parliamentary committee is about to finalize its report on recommended amendments to a bill. For government officials, the right time may be just before an

inter-departmental meeting where several departments are set to discuss the issue and come up with a
common approach to present to their ministers.

A case in point is the events leading up to the 2003
cabinet decision to amend the Patent Act. Advocacy
organizations played a critical role in recognizing the
right timing, seizing an opportunity, and making
themselves available to work with the government to
advance their issue. For years, citizens' organizations
around the world had worked to build a broad public
awareness campaign on the issue of providing anti-
retroviral treatment for the five and a half million
people in developing countries who need it. Major
pharmaceutical companies, generic drug companies,
and a host of citizens' groups were engaged in heated
debate on whether to shorten certain patents to allow
generic drug companies in developed countries to
make cheaper copies of select drugs for export. At the
World Trade Organization (WTO) meeting in 2003,
developed countries agreed to waive specific provisions of the Agreement on Trade-Related Intellectual
Property Rights (TRIPS) that prevented developing
countries from importing cheaper, generic copies of
the drugs they need to treat diseases such as HIV/AIDS,
tuberculosis, and malaria.[1]

---

[1] For years, organizations such as Médecins Sans Frontières had
argued that TRIPS prevented poorer nations from importing
generic versions of these drugs because production and export in
the developed countries that produced them were limited by
powerful patents that protected the intellectual property of major
pharmaceuticals.

After years of discussion, international advocates had essentially pushed WTO members to recognize that public health concerns must override commercial interests when it came to emergency situations. Although internationally countries had agreed in principle, the next step was to have them draft domestic legislation to remove restrictions and turn their public commitments into reality at home.

In Canada, the issue was how to amend our own patent act to allow Canadian generic drug companies to start producing critical drugs for export. Pharmaceutical giants lobbied hard to frame the amendments as narrowly as possible to protect their patents and prevent what they feared would be a trend toward the erosion of intellectual property rights. At least four government departments were involved, with some officials trying to block the amendments and others trying to push them through.

It came down to a critical decision at cabinet. It was clear that there would not be a unified recommendation to the prime minister to go ahead. There was an expectation that the Trade minister was going to continue to raise objections at cabinet. Recall that when a lead minister raises objections to a proposal in cabinet, it is unlikely to pass.

From the perspective of the Department of Foreign Affairs, the minister was in a unique position to make the right arguments at cabinet to tip the balance in favour of going through with the amendments. He needed to present a larger picture of the issue and emphasize the broader implications of not making the change. But to do this required a respected outside voice to echo and support the minister's arguments. He needed to present Canada's international reputation and the impact this decision would have on other countries around the world.

At the time I was working as a human rights adviser to the minister. We had less than a day before the cabinet meeting was to take place. I was scheduled to take a flight with the minister to make the cabinet meeting that evening. After conferring with the minister's chief of staff, I contacted Kofi Annan's office to see if the secretary general would call the minister, just before the cabinet meeting, to bolster the minister's position before he went through the door. Drawing on both the department and trusted advocates from outside organizations with expertise on the issue, I drafted a memo along the following lines:

- Canada prides itself on being a leader on international humanitarian issues.
- Our reputation, however, is based on old steam. It has been years since Canada played a leading role in a major human rights issue and here is an opportunity to regain our stature.
- Introducing an act to amend the patent law would make Canada the first country in the world to make good on the promises made at the WTO.
- The law should go as far as possible to maximize the number of drugs that would be available for export.

- This is a critical issue that could save millions of lives.
- Taking the first step could encourage other countries to do the same and reinforce Canada's role as a humanitarian leader in the world.

What was critical was that outside advocates were sensitive to the political context in which the decision was taking place. They made themselves available for quick and repeated consultation and were able to provide the specific information we needed at a crucial turning point.

The memo was faxed to Kofi Annan's aide in New York. I grabbed the flight to Toronto with the minister, and on the ferry coming across from the airport, the cellphone rang and it was Kofi Annan asking to speak with Minister Graham. We both sat and listened while Mr. Annan read the points in our memo back to the minister. The minister then jumped in a cab, made the cabinet meeting, and was able to say that he had just got off the phone with the secretary general of the United Nations who had made some important points he thought should be considered.

Cabinet decided to go ahead with amendments to the Patent Act to allow generic companies to begin making cheaper copies of certain drugs for export. The issue, of course, is far from resolved. Loopholes need to be closed and incentives need to be provided before Canadian companies can begin to play a part in supplying critical drugs in emergency situations. But the 2003 Canadian decision to amend our law

"Make sure your issue is plausible politically."
John Mackay, M.P., Scarborough-Guildwood, Ontario

was nonetheless important. We were the first developed country in the world to set the precedent of implementing the commitments of the WTO. After our decision, other countries followed, including the European Union announcing its decision to adopt a similar regulation. The 2004 amendments to the Patent Act were just one step, but it was an incremental step in the right direction.

When advocates are sensitive and responsive to internal timelines, it can yield great progress and change. This chapter will help you identify good timing for your advocacy activities, no matter how small-scale or limited your resources may be. Great efforts can go for naught if they miss a key opportunity; similarly, one meeting or call at a strategically placed moment can have great effect. No matter how many resources you have to put in, researching and creating a timeline to help you understand the context in which your efforts are taking place will help you use your resources when it makes the most sense to do so.

Why should you accommodate the government's timing? You don't want to fight battles that do not need to be fought. Designing your strategy around a timeline will allow you to take advantage of opportunities where your issue has a much better chance of seeing progress. Working with the political context rather than against it will help you to focus your energy on how to get it done rather on how to simply get noticed.

Creating a timeline will also help you to choose the best tactics for promoting your issue. You will be able to more clearly mark your progress and measure results. By identifying *what* the most important opportunities are and *when* they occur, you can concentrate your resources on tactics that will have the strongest impact at a particular time. It will help you decide whether a few well-placed meetings, a press conference, or a large-scale demonstration will have the most impact for your issue.

Of course, there are causes for which these opportunities may never come. Working with a timeline does not mean that you shouldn't try something unless the stars are perfectly aligned. One of the biggest obstacles that advocates face is the struggle for attention, or "political will," to address an unpopular issue. A forgotten humanitarian crisis like the one in the south of Sudan (beyond Darfur) is just one example where the struggle is to put a new issue on the agenda. Here your goal is not to identify a window of opportunity, but to shift the government's focus to a new priority.

Even when there is no political momentum, timing is very important. If you plan to organize just one public awareness event, for instance, a well-informed timeline will help you to magnify the impact of your efforts by coordinating the timing of your event with other domestic or international events on similar issues. The key is to find a hook that links your issue to an event that is politically unavoidable so that politicians have no choice but to comment on your issue publicly. Once in the public eye, you can work to sustain the public pressure needed to support serious policy advocacy on the inside.

To begin, your schedule should be based on the time frame you are willing to devote to working on this issue. Can you give it a lot of attention for six months? One day a week for a year? At this stage, the amount of daily or weekly time spent is less important than longevity. Policy issues usually develop over a number of months (sometimes years) so what is important at the outset is how long you can stick with it. Whatever your time frame, that should form the basic line around which you plot all other important events and activities.

WHAT DO I PUT ON MY CALENDAR?

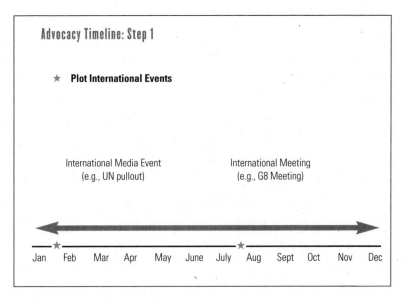

International Events

The first step is to look ahead to the coming year and identify all possible international events that are relevant to your issue. These are represented by the stars (⋆).

International Meetings

Knowing the date of international meetings allows you to infer a lot of information. G8 summits, sessions of the UN Security Council, specific meetings of UN committees, or the General Assembly of the OAS (Organization of American States) are all examples of international meetings that require a whole series of activities and decisions to be undertaken by government departments. Whether a decision is required or not, we know that before they arrive at meetings, national governments have to have a general idea of how they will vote on the major issues and what their positions will be.

So what does this tell you? Look for international events that are relevant to your issue. You can infer that there will have to be a series of decisions made before that event arrives. If the issue is of national importance, it is likely that the issue will have to go to cabinet. If it falls within the jurisdiction of one department, you can assume that it will be presented in a formal memo to the relevant minister for decision. If it is a routine matter that is regularly discussed at an international committee, the decision will most likely be made at the level of officials by a deputy minister, assistant deputy minister, or an ambassador.

The dates of these meetings are usually available on main Web sites of international organizations. A broad outline of the agendas is usually posted in advance. To figure out which international meetings are significant for you, begin by looking at the UN home page for relevant UN Security Council, General Assembly, and committee meetings. Next browse the Web sites of international regional organizations such as ASEAN (the Association of Southeast Asian Nations), OAS (the Organization of American States), the African Union (AU), or the European Union. Finally, major political meetings or summits between leaders can also be important. These include G8, the G-20, NAFTA meetings, or bilateral summits between just two international leaders on a significant issue.

Knowing the specific date of an international meeting can also allow you to make a number of other assumptions about what's going on within government departments. To start, you can assume that when a date for a meeting is set, all appropriate bureaus within the relevant departments will be preparing a host of documents for the person (or team) who will be representing Canada at that meeting. Whether the minister goes personally or Canada is represented by a deputy minister or lower-level official, our representative will receive a series of briefing notes and "talking points," laying out Canada's position on the relevant issues.

For advocates, this period of preparation for international meetings is very important. One strategy is to meet with officials beforehand so you can contribute to the documents prepared for Canadian representatives and influence how an issue is presented. The run-up to an international meeting is often when the battle on framing takes place. As discussed in Chapter 8, how an issue is framed is everything. If you can help shape the language used to describe an issue, you can help define the debate. A well-timed meeting with the bureau "holding the pen" can offer you the opportunity to have an impact on the narrative used to describe a sensitive issue and ultimately the position taken by the government to represent Canada's views to the world.

If a politician is representing Canada at an international meeting, another strategy is to meet with the minister and/or their staff just before the trip takes place. Knowing that the trip itself will make certain issues a priority, you can offer to brief the minister with a public perspective so they won't be caught off guard. A meeting with a minister, timed just before a trip, presents a good opportunity to supplement the information the minister is getting from the department with information from a different point of view.[2]

At a minimum, it is worthwhile to plot significant international meetings on your work plan simply as a reminder that this will be a major source of distraction for many officials. If you're having trouble getting any response from officials on some of your advocacy requests, it could be because they are in the midst of preparations for a significant international meeting.

---

[2] See Chapter 4 for more information on working both top-down and bottom-up simultaneously.

International Media Events

In addition to plotting international meetings on your timeline, it is also a good idea to put *international media events* on your timetable. For example, if there is an expected UN pullout of a conflicted region around a certain time, it is safe to assume there will be international media coverage of a whole set of related issues around that date. This information can be very useful. If you know the international press is following a story, it presents a good opportunity to do domestic media work or organize public awareness activities around the same time. National press is usually interested in covering the "local" angle of an international event so tying the timing of your domestic media work (press releases, speeches, conferences) to international events can allow you to maximize your exposure using the same amount of resources.

Similarly, if you know that a big international media event is coming up (anything from the Olympics to an important Security Council vote), begin your public education or public awareness activities beforehand. Catching the momentum of international attention on the issue can help build wider public support for your cause. Together, the international and domestic pressures will set a good stage to present specific policy proposals at a later date when the time is right.

Looking at the simple example in the above graph, an expected UN pullout of a volatile region in mid-January allows for lots of time to build broader public awareness of your issue and keep the discussion going over the winter. By mid-June you can expect officials to be preparing for announcements to be made at the G8 summit in mid-July. These two events alone therefore give you a good sense of when to make your case. With the anticipation that they may be called to comment, elected representatives and officials will be under pressure to come up with an official statement or response. They will want to gather information from informed groups. More importantly, they will want to gauge the reaction to proposed announcements with outside groups in advance. Therefore, late spring and early summer would be the best time to make specific policy recommendations related to your issue. Even only two meetings, one with officials in late spring and one with a politician in early summer, can be the best use of your resources.

Even if your issue is not related to the set agenda of an international meeting or a well-known international event, plotting these activities can still be useful. Together they provide the international political context in which your advocacy efforts are taking place. It will help keep you informed as to where the government's attention is so that your interventions can be timed and framed accordingly.

Domestic Events

The core of your timeline should be built around identifying important domestic events. These are represented by the stars (★) on the graph on the next page.

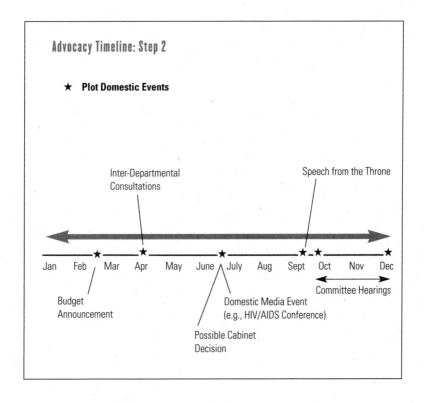

Advocacy Timeline: Step 2

★ Plot Domestic Events

Inter-Departmental Consultations

Speech from the Throne

Jan   Feb   Mar   Apr   May   June   July   Aug   Sept   Oct   Nov   Dec

Committee Hearings

Budget Announcement

Domestic Media Event (e.g., HIV/AIDS Conference)

Possible Cabinet Decision

The Speech from the Throne

Start with the most important statement of government policy each year: the Speech from the Throne. The speech is usually read after the commencement of Parliament at the end of the summer vacation. In late summer and early fall, officials are generally working on developing and framing the language to convey the government's commitments for the coming year in keeping with the allocations set out in last year's budget. Many activists choose to focus on the speech as an important time for advocacy. Getting a reference to your issue in the Speech from the

Throne can be used as a hook throughout the year to see that the government follows up on its public commitments.

The Budget Announcement

On the graph opposite the budget is represented as a single point in time, the date of the public announcement. In reality, the budget cycle can be broken down into a series of key dates throughout the year that include the tabling of the Main Estimates, the release of budget consultation papers, the tabling of Departmental Performance Reports, and cabinet deliberations on budgetary priorities.[3]

For our purposes here, it is important to reference the main events in the budget cycle. This will sketch out the bureaucratic context in which your advocacy efforts will be taking place. The approximate date of the budget announcement allows you to infer some key information: when departments are preoccupied with securing funds for new and existing programs; when the political fight to designate priorities is taking place; and when cabinet decisions on items requiring new money are likely to be made. The Main Estimates and the departmental performance reports also give you a good idea of how money is currently spent and where new funds are likely going. Plotting a rough timeline on the budget cycle will therefore help you gauge when to make arguments

---

[3] See Chapter 5 for a detailed discussion of the budget cycle and strategies on advocating for issues that require new money.

for new money and when to focus on pushing for a reallocation of existing funds.

Parliamentary Hearings

The parliamentary Web site at www.parl.gc.ca is a good resource to help you identify when parliamentary activities related to your issue are coming up. On the Web site you can track the activities of the main standing committee responsible for your issue, the main bills related to your cause, and any caucus committees that may be interested in your topic. The site is easy to use and provides a good navigating tool for those viewing it for the first time.

Plotting the main parliamentary events will help you decide when it is a good time to meet with the politicians. It will also give you the information you need to know about what the politicians are currently working on and which issues are top of mind. Parliamentary activities set the domestic political context in which your advocacy activities will take place. At a minimum, you will understand where the current political focus is and why M.P.s are preoccupied.

In some cases your advocacy goal may be to generate parliamentary hearings on an issue that has been too long ignored. Here it may be a good idea to plot what the relevant standing committee is currently planning to look at so that you can see whether there is a potential link to your issue of concern. If there is no apparent link, plotting the existing schedule will

"When you know an issue is going through the House, contact M.P.s and senators simultaneously. Don't wait until you are in crisis mode."

Senator Raynell Andreychuk

give you an idea of when to push for a new hearing and who may be interested in helping you do just that.

Possible Cabinet Decisions

Although the exact timing of a cabinet decision is confidential, it is possible to infer the approximate time that a decision needs to be made. To make an educated guess about when an issue will go to cabinet, use the international and domestic events that you have plotted as a guide. You know, for instance, that commitments to the G8 will have to go to cabinet before the representative arrives at the international meeting. Usually the decision is made pretty close to the event itself because with ongoing changes, governments cannot do things too far in advance. Negotiations on the final decisions for public announcements often take place right up until the last moment.

Making an educated guess about when an issue will go to cabinet will help you decide when to meet with a minister, whether he or she is the lead minister on the file, and which other ministers may have a chance to give their opinion before a final decision is made. If your topic is related to trade, for instance, the minister of International Trade will take the lead, but there will be opportunities for at least the minister of International Cooperation and the minister of Foreign Affairs to have a say as well.

This knowledge is useful in a number of ways. If your intention is to block a proposal from being approved, you will have an idea of who at the cabinet table is likely to share your concerns and who has an opportunity to raise questions when it counts. If your goal is to support a proposal to be presented, you can time your meetings and media activities to provide the best support you can.

Plotting the approximate timing of a cabinet decision can also be useful in planning the timing of a meeting with officials. If you know that an issue has to go to cabinet by a certain date, you can plan to meet officials a month or so in advance to try to feed into the Memorandum to Cabinet going to the minister for decision.[4]

Internal and External Consultations

It is always helpful to get as much information as possible about when internal consultations will take place as another indicator of a good time to approach officials with your issue. Officials are often open about the procedures they have to go through to authorize a particular decision. If you know the approximate date of when your issue will be discussed internally, you can work to prepare internal advocates beforehand in order to strengthen their hand during departmental discussions. If no information about the timing of internal consultations is forthcoming, you can make an educated guess about when they will occur. In our example above, if we know that the G8 meeting is mid-July, we can guess that all anticipated decisions

> "Listen for clues on timing. When an official says, 'This would be a good time' it probably means they are working on a draft policy for consideration."
> Official, Canadian International Development Agency

---

[4] For more information on memorandum to Cabinet see Chapter 4, "What Do You Need to Know?"

for public announcement will have to go to cabinet in late June (or early July at the latest). You can assume that to have the decisions ready for cabinet, inter-departmental consultations on the issues will have to take place sometime in early spring.

It is also useful to plot the timing of any formal government opportunities to participate in policy development related to your cause. When a department calls for public input through the announcement of formal governmental consultations, it is always a good idea to respond if you can. If you help officials with their work when they need it, they will be more likely to help you with yours at a later date.

Special Holidays or Commemorative Events
It may also make sense to tie your advocacy activities to special holidays or commemorative events. For example, March 21 is the International Day for the Elimination of Racism. June 21 is National Aboriginal Day in Canada. With other public awareness activities taking place, these dates can present an opportunity to approach politicians and officials who may be preparing announcements to address the issue.

Choosing Your Tactics

Once you have created your basic timeline – the amount of time you intend to devote to your issue complete with the key international and domestic events that will occur during that time – you are ready to choose the advocacy tactics that can best advance your cause.

Building on our two previous examples, below is a sample work plan with an indication of when advocacy tactics should generally take place. The example is for a medium-intensity campaign, that is, a campaign that includes approximately three meetings with government officials, one meeting with a minister, two public awareness events, two meetings with an M.P., and one appearance at standing committee, for a total of eight advocacy activities over the course of one year. Remember that depending on your availability and the availability of those you work with, your timeline can begin in September or at whatever time is convenient for you.

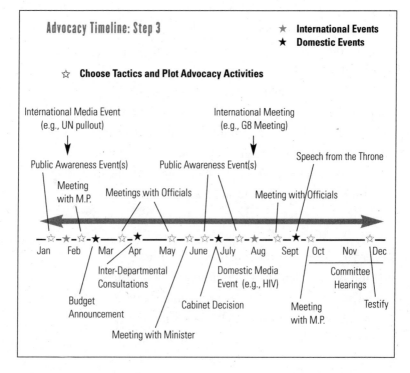

Public Awareness Event: Here the first public awareness event is planned to coincide with a significant international media event that is likely to garner broader public attention. It also occurs before any meetings with M.P.s or officials in order to try to get media coverage beforehand. As discussed in Chapter 3, raising public awareness on any issue is usually a long-term project. Building on the momentum of months or years of work to make something a public issue will support your work to change specific policies later on.

Meeting with an M.P.: As discussed in Chapter 10, meetings with M.P.s should be scheduled well before the budget announcement if your objective is to propose a policy that requires new money. In this case, a meeting with an M.P. is scheduled after a public awareness event (which hopefully garnered some media attention) but before the budget decision in order to catch the M.P. at a time when the issue is most likely to be top of mind. It can also be useful to meet with an M.P. just after a relevant domestic media event when they are more likely to hear about the issue in their riding.

Meetings with Officials: Meetings with government officials are scheduled both before and after inter-departmental consultations. Meeting with officials in advance of an inter-departmental meeting can help you support internal advocates by helping them with what they need to make a case to other government

> "Don't pester officials and politicians. Meet only when it is necessary or strategic to do so."
> Elizabeth Finney, Former Political Adviser to Ministers, M.P.s, and PMO

177

departments. If possible, meet with officials after the consultations. These meetings provide an opportunity to follow up with contacts and gauge where any internal opposition may be coming from.

Also note that meetings with officials are scheduled before a meeting with the minister. This sequence is critical to give you a sense of where officials are coming from so you can anticipate the kind of brief the minister will be getting prior to your meeting. If you can also gain a sense of where other departments are coming from during your meetings with officials, you can prepare your brief for the minister accordingly.

Meetings with officials are also planned well in advance of an anticipated cabinet decision. This allows for the possibility you can have an influence on the memo that will go to cabinet ministers for decision. In this case, a cabinet decision can be anticipated in late June or early July because we know that the government will need to make an announcement at a summer meeting of the G8.

Additional Public Awareness Activities: A good time to hold a second public awareness event is just before the anticipated cabinet meeting. Media publicity prior to a cabinet meeting will help spark the interest of other ministers and draw political attention to the issue at the right time.

Alternatively, a second public awareness event could be scheduled to coincide with a major domestic media event. In this case, the International HIV/AIDS

Conference presented an opportunity to highlight several issues in the press.

Meeting with a Minister: A meeting with a minister should be scheduled just before the anticipated cabinet decision but not too far in advance. Given the volume of issues on the minister's desk, it is best to approach him when there is a reason for the issue to become a priority. If you can anticipate that a minister will be presenting an issue to cabinet (or play a central role in bringing the issue for discussion), you know he will be receiving a departmental brief on the issue in the weeks prior to the discussion. Following up with the minister after your meetings with officials will allow you to present an alternative brief and address any anticipated concerns in advance.[5] The meeting with the minister is also scheduled after public awareness events to build on the momentum created by any media attention.

Additional Meetings with M.P.s: In this case, an additional meeting with an M.P. is scheduled just prior to the standing committee hearings on the issue of concern. Once again, if there is no parliamentary activity on your issue, your strategy may be to convince M.P.s (and the chair of the committee) to start to look at the topic in more detail. Presentations to relevant caucus committees and building coalitions with groups

---

[5] For more information on meeting with ministers, see Chapter 10, "What Happens When We're Face-to-Face?"

that span several ridings are both good strategies to encourage M.P.s to take up an issue in committee.

Additional Meetings with Officials: Here additional meetings with officials are scheduled just before the fall Speech from the Throne. For major issues, it can be a good idea to work toward getting a reference to your cause in the government's public statement of its commitments for the year.

Testifying Before Committee: The date for testifying before a committee is generally worked out by coordinating with the office of the chair of the relevant standing committee. When you are planning to testify, it is always useful to find out who else will be appearing and when. This will give you an idea of what the M.P.s will be hearing both before and after your presentation. If you can anticipate the context in which your presentation will be received, you can respond by setting the appropriate tone and being prepared to respond to likely questions.

Although this template for a medium-level campaign looks complicated, it can be broken down so that you use only the steps that are applicable to you. If you have time for just one advocacy activity, resist the temptation to do it only when it is most convenient. Planning in advance and being aware of the political context in which your actions take place will amplify the impact of your actions and help you use your resources wisely.

CHAPTER SEVEN

WHICH METHOD IS BEST?

Choosing Your Tactics

One of the most frustrating aspects of working on any cause is wondering whether your efforts are worth it. So how do you know whether the methods you are using are having any effect?

The answer depends on what exactly you are trying to achieve and how well you've prepared before choosing an appropriate tactic. For any advocacy effort, you want to select a combination of activities that can best serve your specific objective, using the resources available to you. Understanding how government works (Chapter 4) and how to identify a good time to take action (Chapter 6) will help you evaluate which tactics are best for your particular cause. Recall the two major goals of advocacy: to raise awareness and to change policy. This chapter will discuss a range of advocacy tactics to help you identify where there are opportunities to pursue both.

OPPORTUNITIES TO RAISE AWARENESS

Within Parliament, provincial members, M.P.s, and senators have a number of means at their disposal to draw public attention to an issue and lend their support to your cause. Whether your goal is to prevent a decision from proceeding, expose flaws in a current government policy, or introduce a new idea, working through your members of Parliament can help generate the public and political will you need to achieve your goal.

Statements by Members

In both the House and Senate, members of Parliament have daily opportunities to draw attention to any matter of concern by making a public statement in Parliament. For M.P.s and provincial members in particular, statements they make in the House are a direct way to demonstrate that a particular issue is important to their constituents. Although the government is not under an obligation to respond to individual statements, getting on the official record can help bolster the legitimacy of your cause.

Motions/Resolutions

Advocates often work with M.P.s to propose motions on their issues. If adopted by a majority vote, a motion becomes either an *order* (gives instruction to members or committees to take some action) or a *resolution* (a declaration of opinion or purpose). At a minimum, motions can be a good way to bring attention to your cause and clarify where the political support or opposition to your issue is coming from. The Conservative motion to recognize Quebec as a "nation within a united Canada" is a good example. While the various parties were scrambling to articulate their position on Quebec, the motion forced all camps to be clear about where they stood.

Resolutions can also be useful to draw attention to an issue that is not currently at the top of the government agenda. Although resolutions are not binding on the government, they are useful as a demonstration of political opinion. In this example, the motion became a resolution on recognizing Quebec as a "nation" within Canada that was overwhelmingly passed by the House of Commons in November 2006. In a minority government, controversial resolutions can be particularly important in stalling or blocking controversial government initiatives.

Petitions

Each day members of Parliament have a brief opportunity to present petitions from the Canadian public to bring their concerns to the attention of Parliament. This period is limited to fifteen minutes per day. To be submitted for consideration, a petition must be examined by the Clerk of Petitions to make sure it is presented in the correct form and with the correct content. During the presentation, members may make a brief statement regarding the petition but no debate is held at that time. Once again, petitions presented in the House rarely lead to a direct change in policy. At the right time, however, petitions can help generate enough pressure to create more political will for action.

Question Period

Each day, forty-five minutes is reserved for Question Period in the House of Commons. Question Period gives all members of Parliament an opportunity to publicly question the prime minister (or premier) and cabinet ministers about their policies and actions. Question Period is televised daily and consequently becomes the central staging ground for the evening headlines.[1]

Every government department has a Parliamentary Affairs bureau designed to follow developments in the House, oversee departmental legislation, and prepare the minister for Question Period. The staff in the bureau spend the morning poring over the day's headlines, trying to anticipate which questions will be raised by the opposition later in the day. Ministers arrive at Parliament equipped with a Question Period book containing suggested answers to all anticipated questions on departmental matters. Each suggested answer will be prepared and approved by all levels of their bureaucracies.

---

[1] The Senate sets aside half an hour each day for questions although Question Period in the Senate does not generate the media attention that it does in the House.

Ministers will also prepare answers to controversial political questions by working with the office of the prime minister (or premier) in advance. The leader's communication team will work with all ministers and M.P.s of the governing party to coordinate their message on the difficult political issues of the day.

Although Question Period is heavily criticized as being no more than a forum for politicians to take cheap political shots at one another, it still has the ability to draw substantial public and media attention to an issue. For this reason it is still useful as way to raise awareness, put pressure on the government, or expose a problem with a current government program.

If you have worked to build credibility and a relationship of trust with a good opposition M.P., Question Period can offer a way to move an issue up on the government's agenda. Many advocacy groups work with the office of a member of the opposition to help formulate specific questions to ask in the House. When an issue is raised in Question Period, ministers and their officials know this is something they need to have answers for. At the very least, a question asked in Question Period will cause several divisions of the department in question to take a look at the issue closely and prepare a public answer. The exercise of preparing a Question Period card for a minister will force a department to make public at least a minimal amount of information.

Question Period can also be used as a tool to work in the opposite direction. By supporting a government

"Once an issue is brought up in the House, make sure the press notices. Public awareness is everything. If it's not in the media, it's not an issue."
Bill Casey, M.P., Cumberland-Colchester-Musquodoboit Valley

M.P. (they are also able to ask questions in the House), advocates can help maintain support for controversial government programs or directions. Government M.P.s often use Question Period as a way to clarify misconceptions about existing programs or address any criticism that may be appearing in the media.

In general, however, advocates should be very careful about how and when they approach M.P.s about Question Period. It is very important to be aware of the potential consequences. Working through Question Period too early always has the potential to cut you off from working-level relationships with key officials inside government who are making daily decisions that pertain to your area of interest. If you are known as a partisan group that may use any information they have to embarrass the government, officials inside government will be less willing to work with you. Government ministers will also be wary and will carefully guard what they say and the information they make available. Similarly, if you are seen as positioning yourself too closely with the government, you risk taking on a partisan reputation and being dismissed by the public as not credible.

Caucus Committees

A caucus committee is a group of M.P.s from the same party who meet regularly to discuss a particular topic. Often government and opposition parties will set up caucus committees to study a specific set of issues. Caucus committees have been convened on everything from rural issues and women's issues to

energy policy and child poverty. Often such committees will invite outside experts and groups to give presentations on a topic to provide outside opinions and
advice. For advocates, caucus committees can offer
another opportunity to raise awareness of issue. They
can be helpful in motivating a specific group of M.P.s
to support a cause and help sway the government to
pay closer attention to a particular issue. Government
caucus committees are significant because they provide political advice to the prime minister or premier
on how to handle specific issues. If there is broad
public awareness and M.P.s are hearing about the
issue in their ridings, a caucus committee can play an
important role as a pressure group for a particular
point of view. If the committee wants to be seen as
active on the issue, they may be looking for specific
proposals to champion. However, caucus committees
can also become a major obstacle if the majority of
members are not supportive of your cause. Often this
happens when a public awareness campaign has not
been effective and members of Parliament do not
view your issue as important for their constituents.

Letter-Writing Campaigns

There are a number of reasons that you may find
yourself writing to a member of the government, a
public official, or an opposition M.P. Whether you
are writing to request a meeting, issue an invitation,
or ask for information, the ability to write a good letter
is critical. Letter writing is effective only if the specific
objective of the campaign is well thought out. What

matters is not how many letters are written but whether the objective is strategic and the timing is right. No matter how important, thousands of letters calling for Canada to "improve human rights in Sudan" are not going to get very far in spurring the government to take some new action.

For many people, a letter-writing campaign provides a quick and easy way to get involved and "do something." Yet one of the most common questions people have when deciding to write that letter is this: Do they actually get read?

Keep in mind that the government's current policy is to respond to every written letter with a written response. Although the onset of mass e-mails threatens to overwhelm the government's correspondence system – some individuals are now writing two to three times a day – so far, all departments still attempt to honour this objective. When an official letter is received, it is sent to the appropriate bureau of the relevant department to draft an answer. All departments have specific correspondence units that are responsible for trying to get as substantial a response as possible. This may involve circulating the

TIP

Upon a cabinet change or cabinet shuffle, many organizations write a letter to welcome a new minister to a portfolio and introduce themselves at the beginning of the mandate. Ministers appreciate positive mail, so it can be a good way to start a relationship on the right foot.

letter through several bureaus of a department and consulting with other departments if necessary. Once the letter has received approval from the highest level required (which could be a director general or the deputy minister, depending on the sensitivity of the issue), it goes to the minister's office for approval. Ministers will have a staffer review the draft and make any changes they deem necessary.

When does a minister see the letter directly? The answer depends on the specific personality and the volume of paper a minister is facing. For the most part, ministers generally leave it to their staff's discretion to decide which letters need the minister's personal attention. Staff will base the decision on whether the minister is going to meet with the authors directly, whether the issue is likely to hit the media, or whether it is likely to be raised by another minister or M.P. If the letter is positive, staff may show it to the minister directly just to give them some encouragement.

When petitions or mass mailings arrive, they are grouped together and a standard response is prepared. The minister will usually see one letter along with a tally of how many similar letters were received.

If the point of the letters is very general, a department will usually respond by giving a comprehensive description of everything the government is currently doing to address the problem. If your goal is to raise awareness or get information, these letters can be considered effective. The government will be aware that there is significant interest in the issue and will share as much information as possible on how it is responding.

If your goal is to change a policy, a general letter is not going to have much of an impact. To make a difference, a letter-writing campaign for this purpose should focus on a very specific request. That request should be reinforced by other advocacy activities, especially work with the media.

Here are some basic tips for writing a letter:

"Don't forget the home front. Why is this important in the constituency?"

Adviser to the Former Minister of Human Resources and Social Development Canada

- State your objective in the first line. Refer to Chapter 3 on SMART objectives for a better idea of how to frame the specific objective of your letter-writing campaign.
- The second paragraph should state who you are and describe your credentials and the source of your expertise.
- The third paragraph should contain the rationale for your request, backed up by relevant facts.
- The fourth paragraph should outline who else supports your view and why.

It is important to keep the overall letter short – no more than two pages. It is also a good idea to avoid lengthy attachments unless more information is requested.

Whom should you send the letter to? Generally, letters should be addressed to the minister of the lead department responsible for bringing forward a decision on the issue. The letter could also be sent directly or "cced" to your local M.P., the prime minister or premier, and any other M.P. who has demonstrated an interest in the issue. When working with

M.P.s, keep in mind that your objective is to get them to raise the issue with the lead minister to demonstrate the pressure that local M.P.s are feeling in their ridings. Another option is to cc opposition members or lead critics of a policy. This will let decision-makers know that they are likely to face increased pressure on your cause.

Mailings and Newsletters

If your goal is to keep others informed to maintain broad support for your actions, money spent on regular mailings can be useful. Putting together regular newsletters has become much easier, less expensive, and eco-friendly with new e-mail and Internet options for keeping large groups of people in touch. These types of materials can be helpful to make a visible connection between you and your cause. However, be careful not to overload people with too much material. Too much information can cause your key messages to get lost.

Invitations and Special Events

Chapter 9, "Who Do You Need to Know?," will discuss how organizing a tour of your facilities or issuing invitations to special events can offer politicians a good way to get to know your organization first-hand. It can also give them and excellent opportunity to hear from people on the front lines. Inviting elected officials for a breakfast or lunch with key people in your organization is another way to make an impression and develop a relationship that may be useful later on. Some groups choose to host community forums to provide a venue for those affected by a policy to speak directly with decision-makers.

Special invitations also allow you to demonstrate your credibility and give politicians a visible image of why you are a success. You can use these occasions to show how your work links to the constituency and the broader community in general.

Demonstrations

Demonstrations are a way to show an immediate and strong reaction to significant events. If your goal is to draw attention to an issue and encourage broader public support, demonstrations can be very successful. A good example is the spontaneous demonstrations that arose to protest the sanctioning of *shariah* law in Ontario. The protests were very effective because they garnered enough media attention to send an immediate message to politicians who were still considering the issue. Politicians knew that this issue would be a major source of controversy and therefore had no choice but to sit down and take concerns very seriously before making a final decision.

Actively organizing a public demonstration at the wrong time, however, can be detrimental to your efforts to affect policy. If you are in the midst of building relationships with officials and working to be included in internal policy discussions, going to the media with a radical message can kill the internal motivation to work with you. This is not to say that you should not keep the option open for when you have tried to work within the system but have got no response. But using the option too early can send the message that no matter what actions officials take to address your concerns, they will never be enough.

Keep in mind that demonstrations are most likely to have the same effect as a good public awareness campaign; they can build public support to strengthen your case later on, but are unlikely to lead to a specific policy change in the immediate future.

Public Education

Public education is an important part of any broader public awareness campaign. In order to challenge a cultural norm or introduce a new perspective on a commonly held belief, it is often necessary to get basic information out there on a complicated subject so that people are aware there is an issue they should be concerned about. Taking on a public education initiative requires a lot of time and resources. As discussed in Chapter 2, this tactic is most effective if it is designed and executed well before your efforts to change a specific policy. If there is no political momentum to bring your specific issue forward for decision at the time, plan carefully how you will use your resources over the long term. You do not want to leave a wide gap between your public education efforts and the active measures you take to change a specific policy.

If you can commit to a longer-term timeline and feel that you need a broader groundswell of public support, spending time and money on public education materials can be very effective. Consumer advocate groups, for instance, are pushing for new legislation to regulate e-payments over the Internet. While fraud and error with electronic transactions affect us all, only a handful of organizations are working on the issue. Here is an example of an issue that could greatly benefit from a public education campaign. Pointing out to the public and the media exactly how often errors happen and how much money people are losing could build a groundswell of support to underscore efforts to push for a new law in Ottawa.

Public education can also be useful to correct any misinformation that is part of the general public consciousness on an issue. Public education efforts can also be helpful in motivating and recruiting volunteers who can be ready to take a specific action at a later date, when required.

OPPORTUNITIES TO AFFECT POLICY

The details of government policy are generated within government departments. To have an impact on a specific policy, therefore, you usually need to get involved early, before an issue is before Parliament for consideration. As an example let's look at how a minister introduces legislation. A minister can introduce draft legislation into the House of Commons as a "government bill" only when it has received cabinet approval. Before the bill gets to cabinet, the minister's department will usually hold some form of public consultation on the proposed policies to be included in the new law. It is during this drafting process that advocates can meet with officials to push for specific changes to certain policies.[2] During the consultations, advocates can present ideas, raise objections, or even offer specific wording to be included in the draft bill. The broader the interest in participating, and the louder the cry from advocates, the more involved these departmental consultation processes can be.

Also during this time, many ministers hold their own meetings with individuals and organizations to get a sense of where opposition to the bill will likely come from, once it is formally introduced into the House. Generally speaking, ministers are looking to head off criticism by responding to public concerns as much as possible and including potential adversaries in the process. Because the minister has the final sign-off on the bill before it goes to cabinet, meetings with the minister before a bill receives cabinet approval can be extremely useful. Most ministers will want to allay major concerns before formally introducing a bill to avoid long delays and amendments at committee.

Beyond legislation, departments are also the central forum where new policy statements are drafted and existing policies are implemented. Therefore, the best time to have an impact on specific policies is before they even go to cabinet for final approval.

---

[2] Upcoming consultations on proposed new laws are usually listed on the Web sites of the relevant departments.

Government-Run Consultations

From the perspective of a government department, consultations with the public lend legitimacy to their recommendations to ministers and show that they are sensitive to the opinions of those they seek to serve. Officials also anticipate that when presenting options to the minister for decision, the minister will want a gauge of the public's reaction at the outset. If officials can anticipate public concerns in advance, they know that their recommendation will have a greater chance of acceptance.

Almost all government departments provide opportunities for formal consultation to members of civil society. These are usually announced through department Web sites or outreach to specific stakeholders who were active on an issue in the past.[3] Many provincial governments, for example, announced formal consultations before introducing a ban on smoking in workplaces and restaurants.

Do consultations make a difference? The answer is sometimes yes, sometimes no. Formal consultations run by government departments get pulled into the decision-making process in several ways. When departments present a formal memo to a minister for a decision, it will include any information on public consultations that the department has been involved in. The memo will attempt to summarize a massive amount of information into a concise document for

---

[3] Recently, Web-based consultations have been offered as a way to offer access to remote communities that had not participated in government consultations before.

the minister's office to review. It will describe how the consultations were conducted and how many people were reached. It will also try to identify trends in what the department heard during the process. Of course, the language of this memo is extremely important. Most political offices will not have the time to review briefs from citizens' groups directly. They therefore have to rely on departmental summaries of the various views to get a sense of where different groups are coming from. In the best-case scenario, a departmental memo reporting on formal government consultations will offer an objective report on the response to a specific policy proposal. In the worst-case scenario, it will downplay negative feedback and emphasize positive comments on what the department proposes to do.

If consultations have been extensive, a department may also include a specific section on "what we heard" in the formal Memorandum to Cabinet. Recommendations presented to cabinet by the lead minister will include an overview of the anticipated public response to the issue at hand. Once again the framing of this section (which is written at the bureaucratic, as opposed to the political, level) is critical. The MC may or may not present an accurate picture of where civil society is coming from.

From an activist point of view, there are good and bad stories associated with formal government consultations. For the most part, governments consult on controversial issues to head off criticism and hear concerns before a decision is announced. When government is consulting only to cover its tracks (by saying that the public was consulted), many groups complain that the options were formulated in advance and officials were not genuinely looking for input. In some cases, departments may have a clear idea of where they are going before the consultations even begin but want to soften the blow before they officially announce their position.

For advocacy groups, this can be frustrating, of course. Some choose to opt out of the formal consultations for fear of putting time and energy into developing alternative proposals that will not be seriously considered.

Regardless of past history, it is always useful to participate in government-run consultations if you can. When a department goes to the expense of setting up a formal process for public input, it is important that groups send the message that they are interested in being consulted and there is a constituency that wants to contribute. When groups fail to show up or to take the consultations seriously, officials may be less willing to meet and hear views at a later date. Ministers will also want to make sure that interested groups have responded to department opportunities for input before agreeing to meet separately and hear their views first-hand.

Some formal consultation processes are effective and do lead to real results. Foreign Affairs, for instance, holds annual consultations on human rights to develop Canada's official positions for votes

> **TIP**
>
> Expectations are critical. Discuss your expectations for what you want out of the process with your colleagues and with officials before you begin. If you feel that a consultation is not genuine or is not being conducted in good faith, raise it at the political level. Political leaders will be concerned if consultation processes are considered biased or unfair before they get off the ground.
>
> Remember that the government is always looking for a "win-win" situation and wants to avoid controversy as much as possible. Although it can rarely give a group everything it wants, the government will always be looking for ways to address hard-hitting concerns and make sure that as many groups as possible see themselves reflected in the final decisions.

at the UN Human Rights Commission. Several of these consultations resulted in the department incorporating specific wording proposed by advocacy organizations into documents outlining Canada's official positions. When governments are genuinely asking for input, consultations can be a great opportunity to participate in the development of government policy and build good relationships with officials that will always be useful at a later date.

When departments are genuinely stumped on what to do about an issue, they may set up a formal task force to examine the policy options and present formal recommendations. The task force may be composed of government officials, independent experts, representatives of non-governmental organizations, and individual members of civil society. A joint task force – in which the government puts together a formal committee of different stakeholders to look at an issue – presents another opportunity to learn more about your issue from the government's perspective and to work on developing plausible alternatives. A good portion of the recommendations made by joint task forces are often adopted. This is because policy options have usually been thoroughly assessed all the way through the process.

Pilot Projects

Pilot projects are small-scale experiments that test out a new methodology or policy. Proposals that have been tried, tested, and evaluated almost always do better than new ideas pitched for the first time. Helping the government mitigate the risk of its investment is a good way to build internal support for your methodology and enhance the credibility of your organization. If you can link a new idea to another model that was tried before, you can be helpful in generating confidence in a new project.

Litigation

Litigation – or making your issue the subject of a lawsuit – is a long-term, expensive tactic, but an important and very effective one. Legal cases that have set a precedent have had a major impact on government decisions. Sometimes the right case at the right time can be the best way to draw attention to an issue and spark action on a whole series of related decisions.

A good example of this is the case of Maher Arar. On September 26, 2002, Maher Arar, a Canadian citizen, was travelling home from Tunisia through New York when he was stopped by the U.S. Immigration and Naturalization Service and questioned without a lawyer for nine hours about alleged links to al-Qaida. After thirteen days, he "disappeared" from U.S. custody, and it was later determined that he had been deported to Syria and tortured without a hearing and without the knowledge of his lawyer, the Canadian consulate, or his family.

A concerted public effort, coordinated by Amnesty International, pressured the government into establishing the Commission of Inquiry into the Actions of Canadian Officials in Relation to Maher Arar. The commission set an important precedent and created a vehicle to review the government's policies on national security for the first time since 9/11. The implications of the Arar case on internal decision-making are still unfolding. What is clear is that officials are acutely aware of the risks of working "quietly" with other governments. National security issues are now being debated in public and through the media, creating a sort of paranoia among officials, who will be fearful of "another Arar" all over again. One acute legal case that garners attention from the media spotlight can cast a tone within government that affects the way future decisions are made.

Independent Research

If your goal in spending money on independent research is to influence a particular policy decision, it is important to ask whether you can provide this research at the right time: before a decision is made. If a finding is brought to light just as the government is considering a decision, independent research can reinforce the legitimacy of advocacy efforts and reinforce your message with credible independent evidence.

In general, governments draw information from a number of areas. Aside from research widely available to the public from university and academic sources, governments commission studies on specific topics of interest. This sponsored research is often geared toward elaborating on the government's existing policies and programs. Individual departments will also draw on studies done by other government departments or other levels of government.

Of course, which questions get asked in a study, who gets to ask them, and how they are answered all have an impact on which options are presented for decision. Equally important are how those options are framed and which options are left out. If you can identify clear gaps or contradictions in the information presented for decision and have the ability to fill those gaps before a decision needs to be made, it can be very worthwhile to put your energy and resources into commissioning independent research.

Research can be particularly useful when it comes from a source that is not easily accessible to the government. Many civil society organizations, for example, have close ties with partner organizations overseas and can provide an "ear to the ground" on a local situation that officials at the embassy may not have. Provided that it is clear where the group is coming from (i.e., its political agenda and background), governments will generally be interested in gathering as much information as possible. This type of information can be valuable to both the partnering organization in Canada and the government itself.

When it comes to written research, outside studies provide one of the best sources of credible evidence to support arguments for a substantial change in a government policy direction. For example, the Expert Panel on the Future of Food Biotechnology created by the Royal Society of Canada in 1999 at the government's request produced a 2001 report that argued the government's current approach to genetically modified (GM) foods was putting the public at risk. Rather than relying on the absence of any evidence to show that a particular GM food is harmful, the report of fifteen notable scientists argued that the onus should be on the government to show that there is an absence of any risk before approving GM foods in Canada.

"Understand that government wants to make a decision based on full information. Don't assume that we know it and are ignoring it. Identify where the gaps are and show us where you can fill them in."
Official, Privy Council Office

Parliamentary Committees

In the best-case scenario, members of both the House and the Senate can introduce a motion asking Parliament to authorize a standing committee, special committee, or joint committee to study your issue. These committees can call in expert witnesses and travel across the country (or even internationally) to investigate and learn about a subject. This is a great way to generate public awareness of an issue. In addition, parliamentary committees play a role in government policy in two ways: by producing official reports that contain recommendations to government on specific policies or issues and by recommending specific amendments to legislation that can be passed by a vote in the House. The government is obligated to officially respond to these reports and, if desired, a committee can request that the government provide that response within 120 days.

In a majority government, the government keeps a close watch on the work of committees. Because the governing party holds a majority of seats in the House of Commons, amendments do not usually pass without the government's approval. Of course, government M.P.s can break with their party and vote against the government, but the tradition of party discipline makes this the rare exception rather than the rule. Moreover, the committee chair will almost always be a member of the governing party. Therefore, there is usually a discussion of whether the recommendations are feasible from the government's point of view before they are formally submitted in the report. The government will generally want to accept as many of the committee's recommendations as possible in order to be perceived as responding to the will of Parliament.

In a minority government, however, standing committees have much more flexibility to make substantial policy changes to government legislation. Opposition parties can join forces with each other to garner enough votes to pass amendments that are antithetical to the government's objectives.

In either situation, the chair of the committee has the politically delicate responsibility of drafting the committee's official report and reflecting the views of its multi-party members. The final wording of recommendations or amendments is an important factor in how the government will choose to respond.

Importantly, parliamentary committees have the power to call in outside witnesses to gain additional information and a broader perspective on government objectives and performance. Witnesses may include individuals, experts, representatives of groups or organizations, civil servants, or even cabinet ministers themselves. This can provide a real opportunity for advocates to both raise awareness of their issue among parliamentarians and affect policy by offering recommendations for the committee to consider including in the report. Whether your goal is to prevent a decision from proceeding, expose flaws in a current government policy, or introduce a new idea, working through Parliament can help generate the public and political will you need to achieve your goal.

How Can I Appear?[4]

The opportunity to appear before a committee is open to all those who wish to express their opinion on an

---

[4] For more on how to testify before committee see "A Guide for Witnesses Appearing before Committees of the House of Commons" at http://www.parl.gc.ca/information/about/process/house/WitnessesGuides/witness-e.htm.

issue in question. To make a request to a specific committee, the key contact is the office of the committee clerk. The clerk is a non-partisan employee of the House of Commons or Senate who advises the chair of the committee (an elected member) on all procedural and administrative rules.

Committees generally select witnesses based on the knowledge or interest of the witnesses, the type of study, and the amount of time available. When committees are not able to hear the testimony of all those who wish to appear, they will receive written briefs from any and all citizens and groups interested in making a submission.

> "You have to include senators early enough for them to be able to take action. Too often, senators are not factored in until it is too late."
> Senator Raynell Andreychuk

The parliamentary Web sites for both the federal and provincial governments generally list all current standing committees and their members.[5] They also post copies of the various bills on the government's agenda and a description of their status in the House.

Tips for Appearing Before Parliamentary Committees

The following are tips taken from interviews with M.P.s from all parties who have been on the receiving end of dozens of advocacy presentations. These M.P.s saw first-hand how some efforts are more effective than others in having an impact on a final committee report. The tips are relevant for testifying before both federal House and Senate committees as well as provincial parliamentary committees.

---

[5] Federally, the parliamentary Web site can be found at www.parl.gc.ca. The provincial parliamentary Web sites can all be found through a link on the main Web site of the province.

1. *Be Prepared*

The context in which an M.P. hears your presentation is extremely important. Those who testify ahead of you and those who testify afterward characterize the environment in which your ideas are heard. For this reason, it is a good idea to get a sense of what other arguments are likely to be made, who they are going to come from, and why. In your presentation, acknowledge what else the members may be hearing and address any contradictions or contentious points in advance.

M.P.s will be looking to you to answer the objections they will inevitably hear from others with a different point of view. Similarly, if you fail to be upfront with any problems or contradictions in your own proposal, you can be sure that others will be ready to point it out to the committee.

2. *Prioritize*

Committees will welcome and expect a thorough presentation on your issue but, as discussed in Chapter 3, be sure to indicate what your top priorities are. If you do not stress which recommendations are the most important to you, it will be difficult for M.P.s to try to address your concerns for a number of reasons. First, they know that it will be impossible to meet all your demands. Taking up the cause of one or two of your issues will be worthwhile for them only if they think it will lead to some satisfaction (and good press) from you. If M.P.s feel that no matter how hard they push, it will never be enough, they will be less inclined to make a concerted effort.

"Be prepared to address the big question: What's the downside?"
Honourable Carolyn Bennett, M.P., St. Paul's, Toronto, Former Minister of State for Public Health

Additionally, remember that M.P.s are facing the requests of many individuals and organizations. Sifting through dozens of recommendations to try to pinpoint the ones that are workable (and plausible politically) is extremely difficult for an M.P. with limited time to devote to each. Instead, they will be looking to you to tell them what the critical issues are and what is acceptable or unacceptable to Canadians from your point of view. If you make ten recommendations, therefore, be sure to stress your top three. This does not mean that your other recommendations should be left at the wayside. Rather, to bolster your case for proposals that are less of a priority, point out the necessary connections between issues to demonstrate why, for example, one cannot be implemented successfully without the other (e.g., we cannot do that without doing this first).

> **"Presenters can be so democratic that their message gets lost."**
> The Right Honourable Joe Clark, Former Prime Minister of Canada

3. Be Specific

Almost all M.P.s agree that a general critique of a bill or policy is not very useful. Of course, if you are against the premise or existence of a bill in its entirety, it makes sense to explain your problems with the general principles. In a majority government, the fact that the bill is going ahead is usually taken as a given. After second reading, M.P.s go into a clause-by-clause analysis of the details of a bill. At this point, the question is not whether there should be a bill, but how to mitigate any damage it may cause and/or amplify the benefits it intends to bestow. A better strategy at committee, therefore, is to make concrete recommendations for amendments that include specific wording that can serve as a first draft for new discussions.

Government departments will rarely accept outside wording first-hand. They will first have to run it by government lawyers and all appropriate bureaus of the relevant departments. When a committee agrees in principle that an amendment can be made, however, new wording from outside individuals or organizations can turn an issue on its head and give the government a different starting point to work from.

4. Demonstrate the Consequences of Government Actions

The more you can provide specific examples of the consequences of taking certain courses of action, the better. When groups speak from their first-hand experience on the ground, they earn the M.P.s' respect and attention. If you can point out glaring omissions or surprising implications of the specific wording of a policy, M.P.s can repeatedly use that example to make their arguments for amending a bill.

5. Strengthen Your Case

Finally, make your arguments from a number of different perspectives. Give social, economic, and environmental reasons that your recommendation makes sense. If you have one particular narrow point of view that is serving only a small segment of the population,

> "Use neutral responsible language to prove your point. Rhetoric and jargon usually rub people the wrong way."
> Raymonde Folco, M.P., Laval-Les Îles

> "It doesn't make sense to bar refugees because they are undocumented. Many refugees are, by definition, undocumented, because they cannot go to the government they are fleeing and ask for a passport."
> Janet Dench, Canadian Council for Refugees

M.P.s are less likely to be able to champion your cause. If, on the other hand, your proposal makes sense from a number of different perspectives, M.P.s have more to work with when justifying a difficult change.

CHAPTER EIGHT

HOW DO YOU GET YOUR MESSAGE OUT?

Communicating Your Ideas

The language you use to describe your issue is essential. Whether you are developing specific objectives for advocacy or running a large public awareness campaign, how you communicate your message is as important as the message itself. For advocates, the particular challenge is to use language in a way that "connects to what people already think, aligns with what they already know and helps them see new ideas in a context that acknowledges their values."[1]

The first part of this chapter will look at how to frame your key messages in more detail. The second

---

[1] This quote comes from an excellent resource for those interested in exploring how to reframe specific issues. The SPIN Project is an online resource to provide accessible and affordable strategic communications help for social justice organizations. For more information go to www.spinproject.org.

part of the chapter will discuss how to develop the most useful means to communicate your ideas to government: the one-page brief. Finally, the third section will situate this work in the context of a broader communications plan that is intricately linked to your overall advocacy plan.

FRAMING KEY MESSAGES

Influential political strategists, such as George Lakoff in the United States, use specific language to reframe public policy. In his book *Don't Think of an Elephant*, Lakoff describes how individuals and organizations can reframe issues, and in doing so, change the way the public sees the world.[2]

Lakoff gives a really good example of what reframing means in practice. Two words – "tax relief" – set off a whole array of assumptions. "Relief" implies that taxation is an affliction or burden that we need to be liberated from. Anyone for tax cuts is therefore a "liberator" and anyone against them must be an oppressor.

But what if we flipped this story on its head and framed tax as an investment? Lakoff describes how the story behind this frame would look:

Our parents invested in our future, ours as well as theirs, through their taxes. Today we have assets

---

[2] George Lakoff, *Don't Think of an Elephant: Know Your Values and Frame the Debate*. Foreword by Howard Dean (Chelsea Green Publishing, 2004).

– highways, schools, colleges, the Internet, air-
lines – that come from the wise investments they
made. Taxation is paying your dues. . . . If you
join a country club or community centre, you pay
fees. People who avoid taxes . . . are not paying
their dues to their country. It is patriotic to be a
taxpayer.[3]

One of Lakoff's most interesting points comes
from his background as a professor of cognitive science
and linguistics. Neuroscience finds that people do
not make decisions based on facts alone. "People
think in frames. . . . Concepts are not things that can
be changed just by someone telling us a fact. . . . If the
facts do not fit into an established frame, the frame
stays and the facts bounce off."[4]

So once established stories or "narratives" become
associated with certain frames, new facts that contradict that frame can easily be dismissed. To be accepted
as truth, any new information must fit a person's world
view. This is why, Lakoff explains, so many Americans
still believe that Saddam Hussein was responsible for
September 11.

In Canada we see the impact of these powerful
frames on the national debate all the time. Whether
we adopt conservative American frames such as the
"war on terror" or create new ones ourselves (e.g., the
"sponsorship scandal" or "same-sex marriage"), there

---

[3] Lakoff, *Don't Think of an Elephant*, page 25.
[4] Ibid., 17.

is an ongoing battle for the language used to describe the big issues of our day.

The volume of work on a minister's desk means that decision-makers have to rely heavily on frames to prioritize attention and resources. Our elected officials simply do not have the time to delve deeply into each issue that comes across their desk. As a result, associations with established ideas and narratives become extremely influential. Decision-makers have to rely heavily on their gut instincts or values, which in turn are shaped by the frames we all share to guide our evaluation of an issue.

Working to frame an issue in the public debate is therefore a very good use of your time. If you can change the language used to describe your issue, half the battle has been won.

Whatever your cause, it is important that you be able to express your core idea simply. Ideally, the best way to develop your key message is to research how people generally frame your issue and then test out different approaches to see how new frames shift policy support for your recommended course of action. Of course, most organizations do not have the resources to undertake such research themselves; however, you can tap in to a number of existing resources to gather basic information that will help you frame your key message effectively. Free online public opinion polls on an array of policy issues are available from sources such as the Angus Reid Global Monitor. Alternatively, major polling firms such as Ipsos Canada, Environics Research Group,

> "Know what the core Canadian values are – like fairness. Tell your story in terms of fairness or a value that people can identify with."
> Carolyn Bennett, M.P., St. Paul's, Toronto, Former Minister of State for Public Health

and the Gallup Organization make some research available through their media links or offer full access to their archives for a browsing fee. Private foundations and non-governmental organizations specialize in helping civil society organizations on everything from developing messages to creating all your media materials.

In general, you want to describe your cause in a way that resonates with the values and needs of your audience but is also interesting to journalists. Your key message should describe the problem, the solution, and any action you seek in no more than approximately 100 words.

"If you can't express it simply, you don't understand it."
Albert Einstein

The Problem

What you are looking for at the outset is the basic frame that currently dominates the public's understanding of your issue. Let's look at an example from the long-term campaign to reframe the discussion on low-wage workers in Canada. A number of organizations, including the Canadian Centre for Policy Alternatives (CCPA), did a good job of understanding general attitudes toward poverty and then reframing the issue of the minimum wage in language that resonated with voters (and eventually provincial governments) across the country.

Early on in the campaign, the challenge was to confront existing frames on poverty that were partially Canadian-born and partially imported from the United States. The existing frames looked something like this:

- Poverty is at least partially the fault of the poor person – a personal problem brought on by bad choices.
- We have to avoid programs that risk benefiting the "undeserving poor" where fraud, waste, or ineffectiveness make Canadians feel taken advantage of.

When deciding how to reframe your issue, start with your specific policy objective. In this case, the objective was to persuade provincial governments across Canada to increase the minimum wage to at least $8 an hour. Once your objective is clear, it is possible to evaluate different messages based on the action they are likely to provoke. Here, for example, if the new frame were about individuals, policy-makers might look to reforming poor people rather than the systems that serve them. If the new frame was just about government and its failings, people might think that nothing could be done that wouldn't make matters worse.

Reframing the problem of low-wage workers living in poverty effectively meant tying the issue to positive images that people can identify with – for instance, the value of hard work. If the new frame emphasized that the problem is about hard-working people who are being treated unfairly, the issue would have a good chance of resonating with many Canadians.

In 1999 the CCPA released a study calling for an increase in minimum wage that captured this new frame very well. Here's how the problem was stated:

B.C. has the highest provincial minimum wage in Canada. But even in B.C., someone working for a full year at minimum wage for forty hours a week will still only make a pre-tax income of $14,872. That's too low. No one working full-time should be below the poverty line.[5]

In forty-nine words, the problem was described in detail and framed in a manner that connected to a broad audience. It tapped into a fundamental shared Canadian value – the idea of fairness. If there is one thing that bothers average Canadians, it is this idea that even if you follow all the rules and do everything right, you won't get what you've earned or you'll be taken advantage of.

In sum, the first step in creating your key message is to try to state the problem you want to address in one concise sentence. This is where you introduce your frame and describe how the issue affects the audience you're trying to reach.

The Solution

Your key message should also contain the solution you propose, expressed simply and tied to values that are widely shared. In this case, the solution was raising the minimum wage to at least $8 per hour. In

---

[5] Note that the campaign to raise the minimum wage across Canada was effective. Not only is the minimum wage in B.C. now $8 an hour, but on January 3, 2007, the government of Ontario also announced that it was raising the minimum wage to $8, the minimum recommended by CCPA.

TIP

It may be useful to think of labels or symbols that reflect widely shared public values. Words like "common sense," "legitimacy," or "unfair treatment" denote a broad message in a few words. If you can evoke mental images or pictures, you are more likely to attract interest from the media.

deciding how to present this recommendation, organizations drew upon public opinion polling that consistently showed that when fears of fraud, waste, or allocating money to the "undeserving poor" are allayed, support for policies to assist low-wage workers increases.[6] Here are a few examples of different messages that were developed to encourage support for an increase to the minimum wage.

- Raising the minimum wage is a way of saying that we value work. We should make sure that workers who are the backbone of our economy receive fair paycheques. (Twenty-nine words)
- Raising the minimum wage is a matter of basic fairness. The wage floor has not been raised in several years so its value has been far outpaced by inflation. (Twenty-nine words)
- Increasing the minimum wage is the best way to fight poverty. Full-time workers would earn an additional $2,000 in wages, enough to make a difference. (Twenty-five words)

---

[6] The Praxis Project, www.thepraxisproject.org.

Whichever your approach, it is important that your solution also be connected to positive frames people can identify with. When people are confronted with narratives they subscribe to, your solution will make a lot more sense.

Request for Action

The last part of your key message should contain your specific ask. If your target audience is the public, your request may be that people express their support for a change in policy by writing to local M.P.s. If your target audience is a government minister, your ask may be that he or she introduce new legislation into Parliament. Any request should be both realistic and possible. Above all, you want to avoid giving people the impression that no matter what they do, it won't make a difference.

Remember that all three parts of your key message paragraph should amount to no more than about 100 words. Once you have a draft down on paper, brainstorm getting it down even further to one or two sentences that capture the essence of your message. The shorter your message, the easier it will be to create concise seven- to twelve-second "sound bites" that can be used for media purposes.

To get your message across, be sure to designate a good spokesperson. The most knowledgeable person in your organization may not be the best communicator. Choose someone with good public-speaking skills who is comfortable in tense situations and on camera.

THE IMPORTANCE OF A ONE-PAGE BRIEF

For advocacy purposes, the most useful way to communicate your message is through a one-page brief. Building on your key message, the one-page brief aims to get all the necessary background information on your cause down to one or two pages at most so that your idea can be read and easily digested by others. Although you may need to tailor your message to different audiences, the overall content should remain the same. You may feel that one page is overly simplified and can't possibly capture the complexity of your issue, but the reality is that many of the people you'll target in advocacy work will need only the core information to do their part to take the issue forward. What happens if it slips to two pages? As with a resumé, the risk is that the second page may not be read by your audience. That being said, if the information on the second page is really necessary to make the best argument you can, include it. A battle for a decision-maker's ear is really a battle for their time. You need to be able to grab their attention, raise a point that cannot be ignored, and offer a recommendation that is both reasonable and plausible.

Of course, if you are testifying before a parliamentary committee or participating in involved government consultations, you may also want to develop a full brief that goes into several recommendations in detail. Regardless of your purpose, however, a one-page brief or executive summary of any policy document you devise will prove to be invaluable for

TEMPLATE FOR A ONE-PAGE BRIEF

Title

(Name of group, contact information)

Summary

- State your key message.

Issue

- Describe the problem in more detail. Link the issue to the government's current priorities.
- Introduce a frame that resonates with shared values.
- Add in credible evidence on the scale of the problem, backed up by reliable sources.

Background

- Give a brief history of the issue using only the facts that are necessary.
- Include a history of your group's involvement in the issue, if applicable.

Rationale

- Explain the rationale for your solution.
- Include any research you have done or provide the best evidence you have to back up your position.
- Demonstrate that you have thought through the major implications of your proposal.
- Address any anticipated criticisms in advance.
- Outline who else supports the issue and what they are doing to move it forward.

Recommendation

- Conclude with the specific ask that is relevant to your audience.

Contact

- Provide the name and contact information for a specific individual who can be contacted at any time for further information.

meetings with ministers, members of Parliament, the media, other advocates, and members of the public.

The brief is essentially an elaboration of your key message. Although there are many ways to structure it, the most simple way is to elaborate on each part of your key message: the problem (or issue), the solution (background and rationale), and the action (recommendation). Remember that in all cases, proper grammar and correct spelling lend a lot to credibility.

WORKING WITH THE MEDIA: THE COMMUNICATIONS PLAN

A good article in the press is exciting. It has the potential to generate a lot of discussion and motivate government to put an issue on the agenda that it would prefer to avoid. But if your media work is not connected to the other advocacy work you are doing, a one-off article risks unnecessarily damaging your ability to build bridges with those in government who have the power to affect your issue. If your intention is not to build relationships, planning is nonetheless important to prevent your cause from getting lost in the next day's headlines. For this reason, a communications plan should not be separate from your policy and public awareness strategy. In fact, your media and communications work should be integrated into your advocacy work all the way through your planning process. Once integrated, a plan can help you find an effective balance between publicly reacting to events and seeking out media attention how and when you need it.

Many good resources are available to help you with the specifics of developing a detailed communications plan to complement your advocacy efforts so here I will just touch on the key elements that a plan should include.[7]

Your Background

It is important to be able to communicate who you are and the role you play simply and clearly. For established organizations, this is usually accomplished through a good mission statement.

> Physicians for Global Survival (PGS) is a physician-led organization which, out of concern for global health, is committed to the abolition of nuclear weapons, the prevention of war, the promotion of non-violent means of conflict resolution, and social justice in a sustainable world.

The mission statement serves to sum up who you are and what you're about in a few words that can be easily included in all your communications documents – from press releases to policy briefs to letters to the editor.

Next, think about the background of your organization more broadly. Who are the people who benefit

"Communication should be a strategy, not a tactic. You can't just say, 'Here's the policy, now communicate it.'"
Kristen Ostling, Canadian Council for International Cooperation

---

[7] One of the best sources for this type of information in Canada is IMPACS (Institute for Media Policy and Civil Society) at www.impacs.org. The Canadian Council for International Cooperation and Amnesty International both offer good resources to assist with communications.

from your services? Which communities do you affect? Are there other organizations that deliver similar services? If there are, is there a way you can distinguish yourself from them? If another organization similar to your own has developed a well-known brand name, you'll want to avoid being painted with the same brush on issues you may disagree on.

At this stage, it can also be useful to think about what kind of image your organization wants to project. Are you perceived as a grassroots group, a radical group, an expert group? If you have a reputation already, is it the one you want? If not, how do you want to be perceived by the media? Having this sort of discussion at the outset can help you choose activities to carve out your own space in the public's eye.

Your Goals

Any communications plan should put your advocacy goals or the goals of your organization front and centre. This will help keep you focused on the task at hand and not get sidetracked by tangents in the media or issues that are not your central priority. Using the guide for SMART objectives from Chapter 3, make sure your overall goals are easily understood. The key message you developed in the previous section should also be included here.

Your Target Audience

Who can give you what you want? Generally, communications plans talk about two types of audiences: a "primary" audience – or the specific person or group you want to persuade – and a "secondary" audience – those who support or oppose your work.

Try to be as clear as you can about who your primary audience is. If you are trying to reach a particular minister, business leader, or politician, give specific names. Similarly, get to know your secondary audience as much as possible. Usually this will be broader, such as "the public" in general. Alternatively, your secondary audience may be a particular group – elderly citizens living in rural regions without effective access to health care. If this is the case, is there information from public opinion surveys on that group's general characteristics? Have they been featured in the media before? Where are they likely to come from and how will they react to your key message?

Strategy: How Far Should You Go?

What kind of media coverage will result in the greatest impact on decision-makers? The decision on which type of campaign to run will depend on the particular issue you want to influence and the resources you have to put into your efforts.

Low-Profile Campaigns

A low-profile campaign would include activities such as one or two articles in the press, a letter-writing campaign, a few meetings with mid-level officials, sending a written brief, and inviting a well-known politician to special events. This type of campaign can be a good way to start because it leaves you with somewhere to go when you want to increase the pressure. With a low-profile campaign, you can build the profile slowly and gauge the level of pressure that is necessary according to the response.

This type of effort is particularly useful when you want to find out more information before going all out publicly with a media campaign. It is also the best way to build relationships with officials and explore policy options that could pay off later on. A low-profile campaign will also allow for time to pursue coalition opportunities that can strengthen your case before raising the stakes.

"People underestimate how easy it is to get an issue on the agenda." Alex Neve, Secretary General, Amnesty International Canada

Medium-Profile Campaigns

A medium-profile campaign is a little more intensive. It may involve meetings with senior officials, testifying before standing committees, meeting with M.P.s, pursuing joint initiatives with other groups, and communicating with politicians or the media. A medium-profile campaign is best when you want to suggest solutions that are well researched and point out the negative consequences of a government action.

A medium-level campaign will publicly link your name with your issue. This type of campaign gives you the best opportunity to offer alternative solutions to policy problems because you can put pressure on the government to act, while still preserving the relationships and space you need to work together internally.

High-Profile Campaigns

A high-profile campaign would include meeting with opposition members, getting celebrities to speak out for your cause, publicly criticizing the government, releasing damaging information to the media, launching an ad campaign, and/or organizing demonstrations.

In some cases it can be a good idea to make a big splash upfront and then follow up with a steady flow of lower-grade activities over the longer term. If you want to prevent an anticipated decision of the government, for instance, a high-profile campaign can be very effective. A strong negative reaction right away may shift the dynamic in your favour with the government wanting to work to appease you as much as possible.

High-profile campaigns can be effective when you want to exert power by demonstrating that you can rally others to your cause and increase public concern. Once you raise the stakes, however, know that it is very difficult to take a step back. For policy advocacy, high-profile campaigns pose a much higher risk of losing access to key people who influence the actual decision.

If you do decide to launch a high-profile campaign, it is important to be reasonably sure that it will result in broader public support. If you launch a campaign and no one responds, the danger is that you will be more isolated in your views than before you began and the government could view you as part of a minor constituency that is difficult, if not impossible, to satisfy.

Tactics

It is important to get a sense of how different media cover your issue. Different editorial boards are known for their approaches to issues that are reflected in how much time is devoted to the topic and how it is generally framed. Read the papers, listen to the radio, and watch TV to see who the reporters are, who covers what, and who may be interested in covering your issue in depth.

In Canada, print media are usually the best place to start because it is the newspapers that usually drive radio and TV coverage. In general, print media have more time and space to deal with issues and they have more capacity to assign reporters to do an in-depth investigation over time. Radio and TV generally have a faster turnaround, with only about eighty seconds to devote to an issue on TV and about three minutes to discuss a topic on the radio. "Chase producers" at radio stations generally read the morning papers to decide what stories to lead with on a given day. Therefore, if you do get a story in the morning paper, you are more likely to spark radio interest.

There are a whole array of materials you can prepare to introduce a story to the media. A typical press kit will include a news release, a background document (no more than two pages), a fact sheet, and a biography of the organization and/or spokesperson. More involved press kits may also include a list of quotes or comments on the issue by relevant experts.[8]

> "Before you meet with a reporter, do your research. What have they written lately? Read the news the day before and know if they've had a front-page article."
>
> Isabelle Savard, Former Press Secretary to Minister of Immigration and Minister of Foreign Affairs

---

[8] Details on how to prepare a good press kit can be found at http://www.impacs.org/files/CommCentre/communications_tool kit.pdf.

Whichever materials you choose, generally it is not a good idea to approach a reporter with a time-sensitive story at 4:30 on a Tuesday, when you know that Wednesday deadlines are looming. Note that for the media, Mondays and Fridays are generally slow news days. Offering an interesting story on a Sunday has a better chance of making the morning papers on Monday. If your story does appear on a Monday, local radio stations are likely to pick up on it in the morning talk shows and seek out the same key spokespeople for comment. Similarly, if your story can "hold," sending it in on a Thursday and stating that it could wait until Monday will help a reporter by giving him or her a reserve of material to draw upon when looking to fill up news space.

Aside from knowing when to seek out reporters, it is also necessary to be ready to react to major news concerning your issue when required. Reporters develop their own roster of contacts on given issues so they know whom they can turn to for comments

TIP

Give a heads-up to officials or minister's staff before you go to the media. If you are doing internal work with officials, you don't want to blindside them if you don't have to. Sharing a copy of a news release or an important report in advance of releasing it to the public will be appreciated and help to preserve good working relationships for future issues that you may want to work on.

or quotes when they need it. All your materials should therefore include detailed contact information for people who can make themselves readily available to reporters on a moment's notice. It can also be a good idea to follow the Canada NewsWire link (www.newswire.ca) on "news releases" to watch out for government press conferences on major announcements. Many press conferences are open to the public, giving you the opportunity to make yourself available to reporters for immediate comment. Be careful, however, to present yourself as a credible source at all times. If you get a reputation as being unnecessarily disruptive (or not reliable) you can quickly create a negative reputation with reporters who play a large role in publicly framing your issue.

How Do You Approach a Reporter?

Once you're ready, the best way to get in touch with a reporter is to start with the main reception desk at the media outlet you're interested in. Sending an e-mail and following up with a phone call is the best way to get your message across quickly. Make sure that your e-mail gets directly to the point. Reporters will skim through it for the essence of the story to see whether they're interested in pursuing it.

Remember that reporters want to build relationships with good sources. Rather than attempting to sell a reporter on your idea, offer to help them do their job by presenting them with a good story. This will be based on your key message, but framed in a way that tells a narrative to connect to a wider audience.

CASE STUDY: WHAT NOT TO DO

Going to the media too early can destroy your chances of a useful relationship and cause you to be cut out of important discussions in the future.

One minister held a public consultation where the policy outcomes were not clear in advance. Early on, after an initial meeting with the minister when no decisions had yet been made, one group immediately issued an open letter of complaint to the press depicting their fears about where the policy was going as fact. The result was that the minister could no longer share thoughts and considerations that went beyond the official government line for fear of being quoted as having made a premature final decision.

On the other hand, two other groups that had diametrically opposed interests to one another chose to refrain from commenting publicly until the final decisions were announced. During the consultations, they continually offered good information and proposed possible solutions. During the process, they had to continually rework their recommendations to address the inevitable criticisms that arose from around the table.

When the decisions were finally announced, both these groups saw themselves as having received big wins. Where they had made the most convincing arguments, they saw their actual words reflected in the final document and eventually adopted into government policy. This didn't mean they didn't also have losses. Nor did it mean they refrained from issuing critical press statements after the government's policy was announced. The timing was what was important. The strategic groups were privy to internal working discussions on policy and developed good working relationships with all involved. When it came time to comment on the government's policy to the media, they were no less critical of the areas that didn't go their way. The key difference was that everyone had a far better understanding of where the different sides were coming from and a respect for other opinions even in areas where they disagreed.

A good story usually contains the following elements:

- *The Human Element.* People are generally interested in people. It is hard to relate to a story that is about abstract ideas. This is why a story on economic underdevelopment in Africa usually starts with "Aba is a hardworking mother of four in Nigeria. Earning $2 a day, she can't possibly afford to feed her family."

- *The Impact on a Larger Community.* The personal story should relate to a much larger issue that gives a sense of urgency to the problem. Including statistics is a good idea if they are easy to understand and powerful. "Aba is not alone. Ninety per cent of Nigeria's 140 million citizens live on less than $2 a day and some 1 million Nigerian children die every year before reaching the age of five."[9]

- *A Solution.* Once again, your solution should be framed by shared values that your audience can relate to. "Microfinance is one part of the solution. Providing small loans to the poor to start or expand a small business can provide the means for hardworking women like Aba to help herself."

- *The Action.* Include something that your target audience can actually do. "ACCIÓN International is a private non-profit microfinance organization

"Media are in the business of looking for good stories. If you have a good story, you are doing the media a service."
Catherine Porter,
Toronto Star

---

[9] Chris Albin-Lackey and Ben Rawlence, *A High Price*, Human Rights Watch. Published in the *Guardian Unlimited*, 9/3/07.

that works in twenty-three countries around the world. Of the $9.4 billion it distributed in microfinance loans between 1996 and 2005, 97 per cent of the loans were repaid. Donating to ACCIÓN's 'Helping Millions' Campaign will give more people access to the capital they need to prosper."

Track and Evaluate

As you begin working with the media, track the coverage you get for your cause and evaluate what was successful and what could improve. As you build a public profile, you'll gain a better understanding of the reputation you are developing and the reaction to your ideas. Tracking your coverage will also help you build a targeted roster of journalists from print, TV, and radio. Over time, that roster will prove invaluable in helping you generate media attention quickly, when it can have the greatest impact on your primary advocacy goal.

CHAPTER NINE

WHO DO YOU NEED TO KNOW?

How to Make Your Own Contacts

There are times when cultivating a relationship with a reformer on the inside of government can catapult your issue forward by placing your information at the centre of government considerations. Although your initial gut instinct may tell you that it is "us" versus "them," it is well worth your time to try to identify internal advocates within government who are fighting their own battles every day in pursuit of similar goals.

At every level of the government, it's possible to find those who share your views and are working toward the same end. At Foreign Affairs and Immigration, I frequently relied on outside advocates I knew and trusted to help me quickly build the internal arguments I needed to make just before a key decision was about to take place. If you can build a relationship based on trust and mutual respect with a well-placed individual, you may find them turning to you for help during those critical moments when decisions are just about to take place.

Contrary to the myth, it is not necessary to know someone in government in order to get things done. Although it can be useful to know an official or politician who can vouch for your credibility, it is by no means critical. Setting aside outright corruption – or dishonest practices such as bribery – even legitimate personal contacts can sometimes be counterproductive.

If you do happen to know an official, chances are that he or she is not the right official in the right department and does not have the power to affect the decision you are interested in. Knowing "someone" in government often leads to months of getting passed around indefinitely between people who have no knowledge of your file and little access to the people who do. Even if you are a personal friend of a minister, that minister still has to take the issue through a system of checks and balances. While the perception is that ministers can often just "do a favour" for a friend, the reality is that they can rarely make a decision alone that can be implemented unilaterally.

If your contact bypasses regular channels, a red flag will most certainly be raised and any final decision made in your favour will rarely be sustainable. If a group is granted funding because their friend in a department or political office uses his position to go against the concerns and objections of colleagues and push for approval of the application, either the implementation of the decision will be stalled indefinitely or the policy will be reversed a short time later. The application may be approved, but payment can be delayed. Inevitably, the friend will move on to a different job and follow-up or renewal of the request will fall to the regular group of officials to decide whether to release the funds. If none of their concerns had been addressed initially and they are resentful that the first decision was taken over their heads, the funding will, of course, ultimately be denied.

HOW TO MAKE YOUR OWN CONTACTS IN GOVERNMENT DEPARTMENTS

Understanding the structure of government can show you how to make your own contacts so there is no need to rely on acquaintances who seem to be connected. A better way to get your views across is to learn how the government works and make sure you are talking to the right people.

Before you start, make sure you have broadened the base of support for your issue to as many individuals and organizations as possible. The wider your base of support, the stronger your case for getting a meeting with the right person, one who actually has the power and authority to bring about change on your issue.

STEP 1: Get a Departmental Organizational Chart

The key to making your own contacts is identifying who it is that you need to get to know. The easiest way to do this is to get an organizational chart for the department most likely to play the lead role in making

decisions on your issue. A basic organizational chart
will look like this:

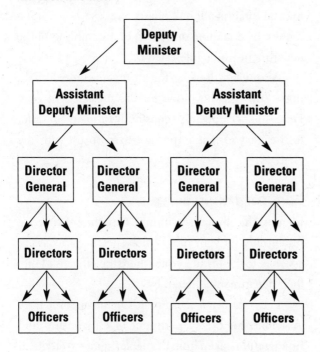

The Government of Canada Web site at
www.gc.ca gives a general list of government departments under the link "Departments and Agencies."
Most departments make their organizational charts
available to the public through their annual reports to
Parliament. They are often included in either the
Report on Plans and Priorities, which covers the stated
objectives and priorities for a department from a one-
to three-year period, or the *Departmental Performance
Report*, which outlines how well the department did
in meeting its objectives over the past year. Both of
these reports are available online either through

departmental Web sites or through the Web site of the Treasury Board of Canada.[1] If all else fails, departmental organizational charts are available upon request by e-mailing or writing to the minister of the department you're interested in.

Also, when looking for an organizational chart, make sure you have one for the most recent year. Departments reorganize constantly from one minister to the next so it is important to keep up with the changes.

STEP 2: Identify Relevant Divisions

Identify the divisions within a department that are responsible for your file. Which specific officials are assigned to your issue? Note where the officials fit into their departmental hierarchy.

Let's look at a real example. On the opposite page is a chart for the Department of Citizenship and Immigration, taken from the department's Web site. If you spend a few minutes examining who does what within a department, it will save you hours of unnecessary work talking to the wrong people. I suggest posting an organization chart above your desk for every department that is likely to have a say on decisions related to your topic. As officials change positions or move on, supplement the chart with sticky notes to keep it up to date.

---

[1] This can be found at http://www.tbs-sct.gc.ca/rma/dpr/03-04/0304dpr-rmr_e.asp.

DEPARTMENT OF CITIZENSHIP AND IMMIGRATION 2005

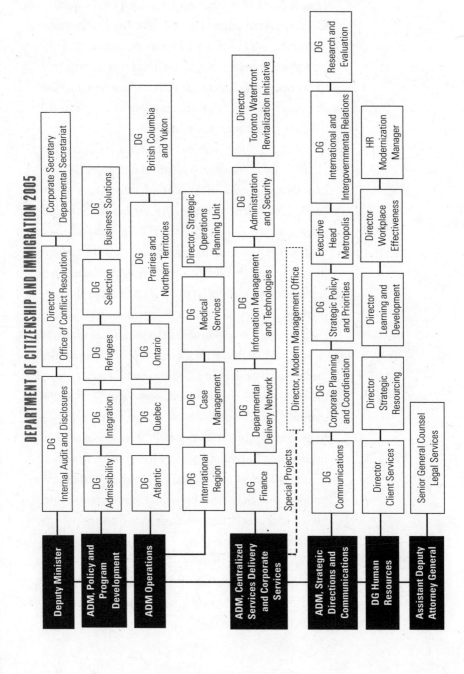

Deputy Minister
- DG Internal Audit and Disclosures
- Director Office of Conflict Resolution
- Corporate Secretary Departmental Secretariat

ADM, Policy and Program Development
- DG Admissibility
- DG Integration
- DG Refugees
- DG Selection
- DG Business Solutions

ADM Operations
- DG Atlantic
- DG Quebec
- DG Ontario
- DG Prairies and Northern Territories
- DG British Columbia and Yukon

ADM, Centralized Services Delivery and Corporate Services
- DG International Region
- DG Case Management
- DG Medical Services
- Director, Strategic Operations Planning Unit
- DG Finance
- DG Departmental Delivery Network
- DG Information Management and Technologies
- DG Administration and Security
- Director Toronto Waterfront Revitalization Initiative
- Special Projects
- Director, Modern Management Office

ADM, Strategic Directions and Communications
- DG Communications
- DG Corporate Planning and Coordination
- DG Strategic Policy and Priorities
- Executive Head Metropolis
- DG International and Intergovernmental Relations
- DG Research and Evaluation

DG Human Resources
- Director Client Services
- Director Strategic Resourcing
- Director Learning and Development
- Director Workplace Effectiveness
- HR Modernization Manager

Assistant Deputy Attorney General
- Senior General Counsel Legal Services

How to Read Departmental Organizational Charts
Organizational charts tell you how the bureaucratic hierarchy works for a particular department. They give you a formal sense of the lines of authority and they also provide a general overview of where files are "housed" – or which specific bureaus of a department are responsible for certain issues.

If your issue has to do with rules for entry into Canada, for example, the chart on the previous page can give you a lot of important information. The black boxes denote the highest-level officials and what they are responsible for. The deputy minister (DM) is the highest-ranking official, runs the department, and reports directly to the minister (the elected representative appointed by cabinet). Under the DM, there are a series of assistant deputy ministers (ADMs), each of whom is responsible for a number of divisions or bureaus that deal with specific topics. For example, under the ADM of Policy and Program Development, there are director generals (DGs) who run the bureaus that deal directly with who is denied entry (Admissibility Branch), what sort of help is available to new immigrants once they arrive (Integration Branch), who is accepted into Canada (Refugee Branch for refugees and Selection Branch for immigrants), and the requirements for entering as a businessperson (Business Solutions).

The chart can therefore help you deduce which bureaus are likely to take the lead on bringing your issue forward for decision. If your issue is housed with the DG of the Selection Branch, you now know the chain of command that will likely be followed for your decision. The DG of Selection reports to the ADM of Policy and Program Development who, in turn, reports to the DM. Online charts are also generally accompanied by a brief description of responsibilities of each bureau, making it easier to identify where your specific issue is assigned.

The organizational chart of a department can help you infer a lot about how decisions are discussed internally. In particular, the chart reveals which other bureaus within the same department are likely to be consulted before a final decision is made. If your issue is primarily to do with Selection, for example, it is logical to assume that the DG of International Region, the DG of Finance, and the DG of International and Intergovernmental Relations will also be consulted. Identifying who is going to participate will give you a general sense of the different points of view that will be on the table and what concerns are likely to be raised.[2]

Finally, the organizational chart provides you with key information to help you identify the specific person who is likely to be assigned to your issue and whom you should get to know. Some organizational charts include the names of the individuals. Others are followed by a detailed description of who is in what role.

Keep in mind that although the bulk of the work on your issue will likely fall to one or two officials,

---

[2] The issue of internal consultations within a department were explored in Chapter 4, "What Do You Need to Know?"

everyone in the chain of command usually has an opportunity to give an opinion. Individual personalities do play a role. In some cases, the high-level person (a director general or an assistant deputy minister) is fully involved and does all the work, no matter how detailed. In other cases, the file is really run by a diligent officer working as a policy analyst under a director who has given them a lot of leeway to work. In this situation, going to the top person may be counterproductive because the boss will wait to check every detail with the point officer before giving you a specific response. When a lower-level officer is the one "holding the pen," the most efficient option is for you to deal with that person directly. Usually the key official becomes apparent after an initial phone call or meeting. If you are talking to the wrong person, other officials are often happy to direct you to the right person because it saves everyone time and energy.

STEP 3: Create Your Roster

If the specific names you need are not included in the organizational chart, it is also possible to find them through the online Government Employee Directory or GED.[3] GED is a complete directory of public servants for all regions across Canada. You can search in GEDs by name or by organization. Under "Organization" you can follow the links down the hierarchy of a department to find the contact information for the

---

[3] To best find this online, enter Government Employee Directory Service in your search engine.

specific official responsible for your issue. GEDs also give you a summary of that official's place within the hierarchy of their government department, including who reports to them and to whom they report.

STEP 4: Identify Other Relevant Departments

For many issues, more than one government department will eventually be consulted before a decision is made final. Although one department will usually take the lead, most of today's major issues are considered "horizontal" issues from the government's point of view. This means they are no longer the prerogative of just one department and one decision-maker. Rather, more than one department will want to be consulted to offer their experience and expertise.

To deal with this challenge in advance, it is a good idea to get an organizational chart for each government department that is likely to be consulted on your issue. The list of government departments on the Government of Canada Web site (www.canada.gc.ca) can help you identify which departments are likely to have an interest in being consulted on your topic before a final decision is made. Printing an organizational chart for all relevant departments before you begin will help you know where concerns are going to come from in advance so you are in a position to address them.

STEP 5: Request a Meeting

To contact an official directly, you have to be well prepared. Officials can't possibly take all calls from individual citizens or even organizations. But learning as much as you can about a specific official's job and areas of responsibility will help you to know when it is appropriate to approach that person directly and how to do so effectively.

When you are ready, the best way to request a meeting is to send a formal letter of request and follow up with a phone call or e-mail. The letter should be clear about who you are, why you want to meet, and the agenda for the meeting.

MAKING YOUR OWN POLITICAL CONNECTIONS

Your political representatives are remarkably accessible. In downtown Halifax, you are likely to see Alexa McDonough browsing at Historic Properties or strolling by the waterfront. People in all parts of the country have stories of running into our most powerful politicians while doing errands in their local neighbourhoods.

It is always best to start with the representatives elected in your area. Members of Parliament are primarily interested in meeting with their own constituents from their ridings. To find the M.P. who represents you federally, enter your postal code at the Web site of Elections Canada, www.elections.gc.ca. The parliamentary Web sites of all the provinces offer links to find your member of your provincial parliament or member of legislative assembly (MLA) for provincial matters. Members generally want to meet with constituents active on an issue because it is their job to stay on top of what is going on in their riding.

Making political connections is really a matter of getting involved locally. Attending town hall meetings, fundraisers, candidate debates, or other events organized by your members of Parliament is a good way to get to know your representatives and to let them get to know you. The Web sites and constituency offices of politicians at all levels are the good places to learn what is going on in your riding and to find out how to get involved. Showing your support for politicians when they try to do the right thing is as important as speaking up when they don't. Fundamentally, politicians are your representatives. If you have something worthwhile to say, they will know that it is in their best interest to listen to you.

Alternatively, you can try to seek out an M.P., regardless of riding, who has demonstrated an explicit interest in your particular cause. Many M.P.s have strong advocacy backgrounds and are known as champions on a specific issue. To identify which members may be connected to your issue, start by looking at the list of parliamentary and caucus committees listed on parliamentary Web sites.[4] Membership in a specific parliamentary committee is usually a good indicator that a member is following a particular set of issues more closely. The same Web sites also provide an opportunity to browse the biographies of individual members, which will often include special areas of interest that the M.P. has been active on in the past.

---

[4] Federally, lists of parliamentary committees can be found at www.parl.gc.ca. The parliamentary Web sites of the individual provinces list the same information for provincial governments.

Connecting with organizations active on your issue will also help identify which M.P.s are interested. Organizations with a long history on an issue will usually know which members of Parliament have expressed an interest in the past.

City councillors are usually even more accessible. For local issues, they should be your starting point to gather information and get feedback on the ideas you would like to pursue. As with members of Parliament, city councillors have an interest in staying on top of the issues of concern to their constituents. If you are well prepared and organized, it is generally not difficult to set up a meeting with your local city councillor.

How Do I Set Up a Meeting with a Politician?

The most direct way to connect with a politician is through their staff. One of the most common mistakes advocates make is insisting on going directly to the top too quickly. In general, it is a lot easier to have a conversation or meet with an adviser than it is with the politician. Politicians rely on their staffers to screen people before they meet with them. If you can show that you are well organized, reasonable, and prepared, political staffers will pass on your concerns directly or arrange a meeting with your councillor, member of Parliament, or even minister in person.

Political staff also offer the advantage of being able to follow up any successful meeting with concrete action if possible. Politicians have to rely on their staff to get information and communicate their wishes (or directives) to others. At times, it can be

> "Get to know the senators' interests. Find out what committees they are on and which issues they have been active on in the past."
>
> Senator Raynell Andreychuk

even more productive to meet with staffers rather than politicians themselves because with their boss's blessing, the staffers will be the ones with the time to follow through on a request and see that it is implemented properly.

To request a meeting, send a written letter or an e-mail with an attachment that includes a good one-page brief.[5] The letter should be addressed to the politician directly, complete with his or her formal title. Explain who you are, why you have credibility, and what the meeting is about. After a reasonable period of time (a week or so), follow up with a phone call to a specific staffer. The names of a politician's advisers are usually listed on their Web site. If not, with your first phone call, request to speak with either the executive assistant or the specific adviser who is responsible for your issue. Your efforts should be directed at the constituency office, if you are a constituent, or the member's office on Parliament Hill if the issue is relevant to that member and you have determined that the member may have an interest in meeting with you (see above). If your request is to a minister, your letter will officially put your request into the department's correspondence unit, meaning they have an obligation to prepare an official written response.

While it is important to make sure that there is follow-up, be careful not to bombard an office without

---

[5] See Chapter 8 for more detailed information on how to write a good one-page brief.

giving them adequate time to respond. The reasons for a delayed response may be legitimate. Often an office will not want to respond until they have something to say. Once your request for a meeting is accepted, staff will generally wait until they have finalized the politician's schedule and have some concrete dates and times to offer you.

The best way to be granted a meeting is to be well prepared. If you have built credibility, done the right homework, and presented your case effectively, you should have no problem making your own political connections and getting in to see the people you need to.

"Find common ground with your M.P. — a regional, cultural, or personal reason they may be sympathetic to your cause."
Bill Casey, M.P.,
Cumberland-
Colchester-
Musquodoboit Valley

CHAPTER TEN

WHAT HAPPENS WHEN WE'RE FACE-TO-FACE?

Meeting with Government Officials and Politicians

I remember a meeting I attended with representatives of very small-scale local organizations concerned about HIV/AIDS. They had scraped together the money to send people to Ottawa only to be met by stone-faced officials and a minister who had to rush out the door. What they didn't know was that at the time Canada renewed its strategy on HIV/AIDS every five years. Two weeks prior, a massive Memorandum to Cabinet had been presented that outlined an array of proposals for federal government policy and requested funding to go along with it. The issue as a whole was not set to come up again for another five years. The meeting was frustrating for all involved. The groups could not understand why officials were simply listing off all the things the government was currently doing to address the issue and the officials were frustrated that they had no levers to respond to any new requests. For the minister, explaining that decisions had already been taken was just not enough. The groups could not understand why their hard work couldn't generate a more substantive response.

Meeting face to face with the right person can be the best use of your time. For that meeting to make a real difference, however, the timing has to be right and you have to know exactly who you are meeting with, what that person can and cannot do for you, and how to run the meeting effectively.

Previous chapters discussed the importance of working on several levels of government simultaneously. To really get your message across you have to work both "top-down" (from the politicians to the bureaucracy) and "bottom-up" (from the bureaucracy to the politicians). This chapter will offer step-by-step guides to meeting with officials, members of Parliament, ministers, and their staff to make sure that your message is both received and heard.

> "Never request a meeting unless you know what you want out of it."
>
> Dan Costello, Former Chief of Staff to the Minister of Foreign Affairs

THE BUREAUCRATIC PERSPECTIVE

Bureaucrats are people just trying to do their job. They chose their career to develop policies and programs that are in the public's interest and to make the best use of taxpayer's money. Advocates too often go into a meeting assuming it's an "us" versus "them" situation. While not all relationships with officials are effective and satisfying, starting off on the right foot will almost certainly get you further than taking a confrontational approach before you begin.

Groups can be very effective when they help officials do their jobs. When an official takes on a new position, for example, offer to brief them on a host of complex issues that you know they'll be expected to absorb quickly. This type of help is often noticed and appreciated. If you can come to be known as a group with reliable research and credible information early on, it can help build a good working relationship that will last through the time the official holds the post.

A good way to prepare for a meeting is to begin by looking at it from the other person's perspective. Recall that public servants do not change with elections. Their job is to provide objective, professional expertise to the elected government of the day. To do so, they consult across government and analyze, evaluate, and formulate policies for consideration by elected officials. Officials are responsible for implementing the decisions made by cabinet and Parliament, enforcing the laws, and providing government services. They are hired and promoted based on criteria set out by the Public Service Commission, not by political affiliation.

The bureaucracy is also a fairly strict hierarchy. As such, most public servants only feel comfortable saying or doing things that are appropriate to their position in a specific department. All officials have one or more levels they have to check with before they can give clear answers to difficult questions. Although this can be frustrating for those on the outside, it is not the goal of public servants to remain evasive for no reason.

From the official's perspective, each level of the hierarchy acts as a check and balance on any information presented for decision. First, public servants have a responsibility to verify that anything they pass on is accurate. Second, they need to know that what they are saying is the official government position. If that position has not been confirmed, they will not feel comfortable speaking on behalf of the government until it is. Third, officials want to make sure that the government is communicating a unified message on a proposed policy. With so many potential spokespeople, most officials want to check that their message is the same one that other bureaus or other departments are giving as well.

Before you walk into any meeting with a government official, it is important to be aware of what public servants can and cannot do. What can they do? They can guard against knee-jerk political reactions to sudden events. They can analyze how a policy could work or point out the reasons it may not work. They can give cost implications and a realistic assessment of what it would take to implement a proposed course of action.

Fundamentally, officials offer institutional memory to the current government in power. Government departments keep records of whether a policy has been tried before and what the result was. When it comes to new ideas, officials will try to analyze all implications of a proposed policy. They will check a proposal against the laws and policies of other departments to see if any implications will contradict other objectives that the government as a whole is trying to achieve.

It is equally important to understand what officials cannot do. They cannot take a course of action that falls outside of approved departmental procedure. Nor can they agree to implement major new ideas or directions without political approval and support. While officials can make decisions that fall under areas of delegated authority, they are acutely aware that many of these decisions can be ultimately overturned at the political level if they draw negative media attention or are not well received by the public.

Officials caution that it is important to be aware of which decisions are political and which can be made by a department itself. For example, the government's approach to social assistance (welfare) is a political decision and not one that can be changed by public servants unless the relevant minister directs them otherwise. Public servants, on the other hand, carry out the day-to-day decisions on assistance cases according to the regulations and guidelines set for them.

Given this context, the range of things you can expect to get out of a meeting with an official is quite specific. For one, officials can help you get more information to understand what the current policy is, what the rationale was, and when the decision was taken. They can tell you how a policy is being implemented and who is responsible for managing specific tasks. They can also help pass on your information to other officials to make sure that your representations are going to the right people across government.

Finally, if your case is strong enough, officials can incorporate your information into departmental briefs for elected decision-makers to make them aware of your position on an issue. Be aware, however, that these briefs may or may not be in your favour.

How Do Officials Prepare for a Meeting with You?

Depending on the level of the hierarchy you are meeting with, officials will look for a background memo on your organization or group. The department keeps records of all past contact with various organizations so your history with the department will usually be foremost in the official's mind.

If your meeting is with a lower-level official, he will usually write a follow-up memo that will go up to his bosses to provide them with some background on you. This memo will contain a description of who you are, where your credibility comes from, which issues you have advocated on in the past, and the concerns you are likely to raise at the upcoming meeting. The memo will then discuss whether your views are in line with what the government is already doing or what it plans to do. It will clearly outline any constraints the department will face in responding to your request. If relevant, it will also describe the positions of other departments and other levels of government. The memo will include any legal implications or concerns with your proposal raised by the department's legal bureau or the Department of Justice. Finally, the memo will contain a recommended response for the official to use in replying to your concerns. This will be in the form of "talking points" that will be circulated to any other official you may meet in the future. If you are meeting with someone higher up, he or she will have that memo in hand to draw on as a main resource.

HOW TO PREPARE FOR CONVERSATIONS WITH OFFICIALS

Chapter 9 discussed how to make your own contacts within government departments. Recall that the first step is to make sure you are speaking with the right person at the right level in the hierarchy, in the right department. Once you've identified that specific official, there are a number of questions you should ask yourself before making contact.

• *Who exactly are you meeting with?*
Drawing on the department's organizational chart and the Government Employee Directory, ask yourself the following: What level is this person at? What is their particular job? What are their specific areas of responsibility?[1] Try to identify what they are working on and where the gaps in their information may be. Also try to anticipate where you may be able to help them do their job. If the official's job is to monitor the impact of a particular policy and you have people working on the ground, for instance, offer them access

---

[1] Chapter 9 contains a more in-depth discussion on how to find and read departmental organizational charts and the Government Employee Directory.

to another source of information to keep them on top of the issue.

● *Who do they report to?*
Consult the department's organizational chart to understand to whom that official reports and how many levels are above them. This will help give a sense of who holds the final authority on decisions that official is involved in.

"Give as much information in advance as to what the meeting is about so that officials can prepare."
Alex Neve, Secretary General, Amnesty International, Canada

● *Which consultation processes are they a part of?*[2]
When setting up your meeting, request information on which other divisions of the department play a role in your issue. Ask if there is an inter-departmental consultation group that is looking at it. If so, who is involved? This information is not normally confidential, and officials themselves find it more convenient to help you speak with the right bureau in order to make the best use of everyone's time. Also be sure to ask whether there are formal public consultations on the proposed policy or what other opportunities exist to make your views known.

● *What specific action can this official take to advance your issue?*
This is the most important part of your preparation. As discussed in Chapter 3, "What Do You Want to

---

[2] Chapter 4, "What Do You Need to Know?" contains more information on internal government consultations.

Achieve?", it is critical to have an idea of what this particular official can do for you so you can ask for something that is possible. Your request for action must be within that person's power. The more specific you are, the easier it will be to follow up.

For meetings with officials at all levels of the bureaucratic hierarchy, your request for action should be very specific. Can this person raise the issue at the next interdepartmental meeting? Can they raise it with their boss? Can they put it on the agenda for the minister's bilateral meeting with the Chinese foreign minister next week? Can they ask this question when you consult with the Arab group on this specific UN General Assembly resolution? If your request is specific and within the person's power, you are much more likely to see some concrete results.

• *What other information can they provide?*
Before you set up your meeting or conversation with a public servant, go back to your research and identify where there are gaps in your information. Ask yourself whether this particular official will be able to fill in those gaps, and if not, who can. Develop a list of questions you will want to raise during the meeting.

THE MEMBER OF PARLIAMENT'S PERSPECTIVE

A member of Parliament is coming from a very different place than a departmental official. A good M.P. or provincial member will want to keep abreast of everything going on in their riding. To get a sense of the issues that are important to their riding, they will meet with community leaders, representatives of advocacy organizations, and leaders of the various ethnic associations. As discussed in Chapter 9, members also meet, when time permits, with individual constituents who have particular concerns.

Most members emphasize that it is a good idea to try to build a prior relationship, before you need them urgently to act on your behalf. Even if you are not a supporter of that member's political party, going to events will help build trust and a credible reputation before going to a constituency office with a request.

M.P.s and provincial members, like ministers, are constantly trying to balance competing interests to try to arrive at a solution to a problem that will have the most support from all sides. The more connected they are to the current concerns and issues within their community, the more effective they can be as the community's principal representative to Parliament. Members are concerned with communicating government policy to their constituents and relaying the reaction to that policy back to the government. Their goal is to maintain public support for both their own role and the role of their party.

Although appointed senators don't have constituency offices, they have many of the same goals as elected members. A key difference is that senators can afford to take a longer-term view of an issue as they do not have to worry about the pressures of the next election.

What Can a Member Do for You?

• *Provide access to the government*
Your local M.P. or provincial member is your starting point to access all aspects of your government. They are your direct link to Parliament and the business going through the legislature or city council. Members will usually be well briefed to help answer any questions you may have about items on the current parliamentary agenda.

Members and senators can connect you to the right government department responsible for your issue. Most will be familiar with specific programs of concern in their ridings, but if they are not, they can get the information to direct you to the right place. Members can also link you up with a minister's office or their staff if appropriate.

Many members also play an active role in assisting with the delivery of particular government services. On immigration cases, for example, constituency offices are very active in working with the Immigration Department and the minister's offices to get a status update on specific cases and help potential immigrants or Canadians sponsoring immigrants understand the rules and requirements of the legislation. Constituency offices may also get involved when an immigration case has been denied. If a member feels that the constituent bringing the case is credible and has good cause for revisiting the decision, they may appeal to the minister's office directly. By law, the minister of Immigration retains power to take a second look at a decision made by the department and can override that decision if they believe it's warranted.

Be careful, however, when you choose to use this system and what your expectations are. Members have to be very careful about the cases they decide to champion because their own credibility is on the line. For example, an M.P. may push the minister to grant a visitor's visa for a person who was denied by the department because a group of constituents whom they know and trust have vouched that the individual in question will return to their home country at the end of the period allowed by the visa. If, however, that individual does not return and chooses to stay illegally, the member's ability to bring other cases forward will be damaged. The minister will not want to risk overriding their department's judgement again, based solely on that member's word.

• *Help you navigate through the system*
M.P.s can assist you in getting answers from the bureaucracy or advise you on how things work. If you have exhausted regular channels (such as departmental Web sites and call centres), M.P.s may be able to help break logjams or get information more directly. They can also help you learn whom you need to meet and where you need to go next to advance your cause.

Members and senators can give you an overview of the larger political context affecting the decisions on your issue. They can tell you where the various parties are coming from and what the priorities currently are.

They can also give you their take on the chances of an issue moving forward at the present time.

• *Raise awareness of your cause*
Members and senators can help raise awareness of an issue in caucus or with a minister on your behalf. If they choose to take your cause on, they can even go so far as to issue a press release or lend their name and reputation to supporting your efforts. They can also call attention to your issue by making statements in the House of Commons, reading speeches at various events, or raising the issue in Question Period.

• *Connect you with others outside government*
Members are exposed to a broad range of organizations and have a lot of contacts. Given their detailed interest in the riding, members can help link you up to a network of people, organizations, and government bodies active in your cause. They can also help build alliances in support of a particular cause or piece of legislation.

THE MINISTER'S PERSPECTIVE

If your timing is right and you are properly prepared, a meeting with a minister can have a direct impact on the decisions they make. Keep in mind that ministers are first and foremost members of the legislature elected by their constituents. They are acutely aware of how proposed government policies are playing in their ridings and want to avoid the political fallout of not paying close attention to the public response.

> "Keep in mind that M.P.s are not involved in the day-to-day decisions of government. They cannot single-handedly drive an issue nor can they make a decision on the government's behalf. It is up to you to build the coalition; they can choose to be a part of it."
> Anita Neville, M.P., Winnipeg South Centre

Before any meeting, ministers will look to a number of sources for their views. What advice is my department giving? Does my political staff agree? What are my constituents saying on the issue? Of course, ministers will ask whether a decision on your issue would be consistent with other things they have said or done and whether it will affect their chances for re-election.

Ministers are appointed for political reasons. Recall that in most cases they are not an expert on their portfolio and have to rely heavily on their departments to give them the information they need to make informed decisions. Some ministers have a lot of experience in receiving departmental briefs with a critical eye while others have very little. Although a few ministers may have specific ideas about what they want to accomplish during their time with a department, their main priorities are set by a *mandate letter*, given to them by the prime minister upon appointment. This mandate letter lays out the specific tasks that the minister is to accomplish during their time at a department, based on the government's agenda.

Aside from trying to focus on their political priorities, ministers are also preoccupied with keeping an eye on the day-to-day management of their department's operations. Question Period is a daily reminder that ministers are publicly accountable to Parliament for all actions taken by the department under their responsibility. They are acutely aware that the media will be looking to them for answers. Staying on top of what is going on in the department therefore accounts for a significant part of any minister's time.

What are ministers thinking when they meet with you? Most ministers will have a number of particular questions on their minds. Why is this issue important now? Why should I devote time and energy to it? How controversial is it? Does it fit with the government's agenda? Who else is speaking out publicly on the issue? Which groups stand to win by this decision and which groups stand to lose?

So what can you ask a minister to do? First, ministers can bring in outside information and different points of view. They can ask that a new idea be formally evaluated through official channels. They can question the material that is presented by departments for decision and ask that additional issues are addressed. Ultimately, if a minister remains unconvinced by the material before them, they can refuse to sign off on the department's proposed course of action.

What a minister cannot do is unilaterally change a policy direction. As we saw in Chapter 4, "What Do You Need to Know?" ministers cannot create a new policy and approve it without departmental consultation, analysis, and evaluation. Nor can they unilaterally implement a decision, even if taken at the highest levels. Ministers need their departments to be at least minimally supportive of a decision to make sure that there is follow-up once the policy is officially announced to the public.

Keep in mind that ministers do not want to be pitted against their officials unnecessarily. They know that it is wiser to maintain good relations with their departments so that they can choose their battles carefully when they really need to.

The Role of Ministers' Offices

Many advocates underestimate how useful a minister's staff can be to them. Ministers' staff range from political party loyalists and people who have worked hard to get their member elected, to experts hired to offer their services in a particular area of specialty. A good "staffer" can be the best source of information in the system. Because they work directly for the minister, staffers get a bird's-eye view of everything on a minister's desk – from all business going on in the department to the political issues dominating government thinking at the time to the ongoing issues within the House of Commons. They are also well aware of the minister's priorities and obligations as gatekeepers of his or her schedule.

Political staff look at the issues to see what's in the minister's best interest. Their job is to evaluate the department's agenda with a critical eye to try to help the minister draw an appropriate line on difficult and controversial issues. They will also view each issue through a political lens: How will the minister be received by the media? The stakeholders? His or her colleagues? The public?

Advocates should get to know political staffers. In particular, it can be very useful to meet with advisers early on, before they have received departmental briefs. That way a group can arm the staffer with good questions to ask. The following provides a quick who's who in the minister's office and what they can do for you.

Who Works for a Minister?

Executive Assistant or Chief of Staff

The executive assistant (EA) is the minister's right-hand person and can speak for the minister in his or her absence. All information going to and coming from the minister usually goes through the EA first. The EA deals directly with the prime minister's or premier's office and any other prominent person on the minister's behalf. Importantly, the EA is responsible for overseeing the minister's schedule, in consultation with the minister. This involves a constant assessment of the priorities for the office and where the minister should focus attention at any given time.

The EA has a crucial relationship with officials in the department. As the guardian of all access to the minister, the EA will first receive and review all departmental documents before giving them to the minister for signature. Due to time constraints, ministers cannot possibly keep track of every memo for decision. Therefore, a minister will usually rely heavily on the EA to anticipate problems, so the EA will work intensely with departmental officials to address the minister's concerns with any memo to be signed. To keep the department running smoothly, the EA will also work with officials to try to see that the department gets ministerial approval for important departmental actions on time. The EA is also responsible for hiring staff in the minister's office and coordinating their work.

Politically, the EA will be in contact with the EAs in other ministers' offices, as well as with the core staff of the prime minister or premier. This keeps the minister up to date with all recent political developments so that all ministers can convey consistent messages on issues affecting the government as a whole.

Policy Assistants/Advisers

Policy advisers are assigned a certain number of departmental issues or "files" to watch over on the minister's behalf. This will usually mean that certain bureaus of a department that work on those files will report first to the adviser before finalizing a document for the minister's signature.

A policy adviser's main job is to read through all these documents with a critical eye so that they can give the minister a heads-up on potential problems. Because the minister does not have the time to read every lengthy brief in full, it is the policy adviser's task to read over the details, ask the right questions, and give the EA or minister any additional information he or she may need to make a decision.

Importantly, a good policy adviser can bring in outside groups or experts to offer alternative analyses to the one offered in departmental recommendations.

Political Assistants/Advisers

Political staff are usually assigned by region. A western assistant, for example, will be responsible for responding to concerns from members of Parliament from the western provinces and keeping the minister informed of political developments in those provinces. Regional political staff may also handle requests for meetings with the minister from groups or individuals from that region. They will speak with the group first, get a sense of the agenda, ask the department for any background information it may have, and then bring the issue to the minister for decision. They will also keep on top of any major political issues affecting their region. So if a decision by the government on Haiti is getting a major reaction from the Haitian community in Montreal, the Quebec staffer may meet with groups on the minister's behalf, attend government meetings to get more details on the policy, and connect with other caucus members to discuss possible ways to address concerns.

Legislative Assistants

The legislative assistant (LA) is responsible for following all the minister's business in the House of Commons. This includes preparing the minister for Question Period, guiding the minister's bills through parliamentary procedures, organizing the minister's appearances before standing committees, monitoring the opposition, and keeping an ear to the ground on inside party politics.

Most departments have a particular bureau devoted to legislative affairs. The legislative assistant acts as this bureau's link to the minister. Answers to Question Period questions will be drafted by the department and then vetted by the LA, who will usually amend the suggested response to reflect political considerations. The LA will also work to prepare the minister politically for all appearances at standing committees or public statements in the House. This means revising speeches and any documents the minister may table for public review.

Press Secretaries

Press secretaries are in charge of communications for the minister. While a communications branch of the department will draft suggested responses to questions from the media, the press secretary's job is to add a political lens to each suggested response and oversee all communication strategies relating to controversial issues. Press secretaries will keep the minister up to date on all recent stories in the news and will coordinate all the minister's public appearances and media engagements.

Correspondence Assistant

Some ministers also employ a correspondence assistant to oversee all official replies to the minister's mail and e-mail. Although a department will draft a suggested reply to all formal letters in the system, the correspondence assistant will read over every letter that goes out with the minister's signature. The correspondence assistant will decide which letters the minister may need to see directly and which can be signed on his or her behalf. In some offices, this task is divided among other political and policy assistants instead of centred in one position.

What Can the Minister's Office Do for You?

1. Get Information

The minister's staff can request any information they may need from a designated departmental assistant who is specifically assigned to the office to respond to these requests. Of course, while ministerial staff can not divulge protected information, they can usually get the most direct answers possible to any policy question. When a staffer puts in a request, the department will normally prepare what's called an information memo for the minister's office. The memo will include information on the history of the government policy in this area, the rationale for any policy changes, and the current state of affairs for a specific policy or program.

2. Identify Bottlenecks

Ministers' staff usually have a good overview of what is going on throughout the department. From the top of the hierarchy they can see how the legislative agenda, the cabinet agenda, inter-departmental meetings, international meetings, and funding decisions all link together. This perspective allows staff to see the effects of certain decisions on other aspects of the government, making it easier to identify where an issue is stuck.

Ministers' offices also manage relations with other departments. To do so, they work to resolve inter-departmental problems before they get to the minister. This allows staff to get to know how other departments view an issue and why. For these reasons, a good staffer should be able to help you identify a problem and suggest ways of navigating through it.

3. Supplement Departmental Briefs

Political staff provide the "challenge function." When they read departmental briefs, they are looking to ask the right questions and make sure that the minister will not be blindsided by an aspect of an issue that has been played down by a department or forgotten.

Political staff have the opportunity to add to the memo information that is not provided by the depart-ment. When I worked as human rights adviser to the Foreign Affairs minister, I would often add supple-mental "stickies" to the minister's notes just prior to a bilateral meeting, a cabinet meeting, or even an inter-national address. A staffer is usually the last one to speak to the minister before an important meeting or event. For this reason, a good meeting with a political staffer can be invaluable for advocates who want to have their views presented to a minister during a crit-ical moment of decision.

> "Advisers appreciate when advocates give them a 'heads-up' on an issue that is about to hit the minister. A warning about how the public is likely to react is always useful."
>
> Isabelle Savard, Former Press Secretary to Minister of Immigration and Foreign Affairs

4. *Help You Get a Meeting and Make Sure There Is Follow-up*

Political staff often act as the gatekeeper to how ministers use their time. They can either take a meeting on a minister's behalf or recommend that the minister meet with a group or individual personally.

How to Prepare for Meetings with Politicians

Political meetings should in no way supersede the work you do with officials. Since officials develop the policies and carry them out, you don't want to go over their heads to the big boss if you don't have to. That being said, a good meeting with a minister can be very effective, if you are properly prepared.[3]

Recall that for most meetings, departments will prepare a specific memo to brief the minister in advance. This memo will contain the sum total of information the department has about you and the issue, signed off at the highest levels.

Keep in mind that all information in the briefing note will be from the department's perspective. The more you know about that perspective in advance, the easier it will be to prepare for your meeting with the minister. If you have had previous meetings with officials, you should have a good idea of their point of view and what their suggested talking points to the minister may be. Meeting with the minister directly is

> "Keep in mind what the minister's staff cannot do. They cannot make a decision on behalf of the minister or department unless authorized to do so in advance. They cannot interfere in the affairs of another department or disclose protected information."
> Elizabeth Finney, Policy Adviser to Former Ministers, M.P.s, and the Prime Minister's Office

---

[3] Chapter 9, "Who Do You Need to Know?" discusses how to go about requesting a meeting with a minister.

your opportunity to present an alternative point of view and pose pertinent questions to the established way of thinking.

When it comes to meeting with M.P.s, the situation is quite different. Members do not have access to the same abundance of information that ministers and officials do. They do not have a large research capacity outside of the resources of the Library of Parliament. Before your meeting, ask the M.P.'s staff how much information the M.P. will have on your issue and tailor the meeting accordingly. In some cases, they will be well briefed on an issue so you don't want to waste time on obvious points. In others, you want to make sure the M.P. has the necessary background to understand why your request is important.

For all meetings with politicians, be clear about your agenda and present all your issues at one meeting, rather than requesting separate meetings for each issue. Know beforehand exactly how much time you have and at all costs, try to stay on time. If your meeting goes off on tangents and makes the politician late for their next meeting, that may be the only thing they remember. Whatever time you have, make sure that you organize it wisely. Be sure to stress your key messages and avoid presenting information that the politician is likely to already know.

If you are advocating for a change, understand what is required of government for your change to happen. Try to be familiar with the laws and regulations

"A common mistake that groups make is to present expensive glossy packages or CDs that contain a lot of superfluous information that is not relevant to the M.P.'s needs. An M.P. will not have time to sift through the material later to get what they need."
Anita Neville, M.P.,
Winnipeg South Centre

pertaining to your issue – they are usually available on either the parliamentary Web site or the Web sites of the relevant government department.

Finally, use fairly neutral language to prove your points rather than using rhetoric or jargon that will detract from your fundamental message. Most importantly, don't forget the home front. Demonstrating why your issue is important in the constituency will make it a personal accountability issue for your -representative.

HOW TO RUN EFFECTIVE MEETINGS

Now that you are well prepared, the following offers a step-by-step guide on how to run an effective meeting with an official, member of Parliament, or minister. Although there are many similarities between running good meetings with officials and with politicians, there are also some important differences.

STEP 1: Start with the Good News

Starting with the good news is very important to establishing a good working relationship from the outset. Remember that officials and politicians are engaged in their own internal fights every day. Although they may not be able to give you all the details about a raging battle within government, you can be sure that most feel as though they already have enough internal opposition on their hands without taking on yet another fight. Nothing can ruin a good relationship more than feeling like your hard work is unnoticed or

"Be strategic about when you ask for the politician's time and attention."
Political Adviser, Industry Canada

"Keep the meeting simple. Remember that M.P.s are interested in the broad strokes, since it is officials who deal with the specific details of a proposal."
John Mackay, M.P., Scarborough-Guildwood, Ontario

under-appreciated. Acknowledging their efforts to date will always be appreciated and will help generate the energy to take on another difficult task.

When meeting with a politician, beginning with the good news is not just for empty flattery. During the course of their hectic days, ministers and M.P.s are presented with one problem after another. If you open the meeting by firing out a barrage of criticisms, demands, or accusations, the politician is likely to shrug their shoulders and think, "Well, there's no way to win this one because no matter what I can do, it won't be enough."

If a politician is going to go out on a limb for your cause, it is important for them to know that their efforts will register with the advocacy community. If you want them to push your issue, they will need a lot of backup and support. Starting a meeting on a positive note sends the message that if the politician chooses to champion your cause, they won't be alone. It conveys that you are reasonable and someone the government can work with.

To get a sense of the person's most recent achievements, read through newsletters and browse the member's Web site. This will give you an idea of what they are currently working on and how they are spending their time.

Once again, it is important to take as a given that those in government want to do the right thing. Assume that they have agreed to the meeting because they want to hear what you have to say and are willing

> "If warranted, speaking out publicly when there is good news will go a long way to building a good relationship. The next time you are looking for a meeting, your actions will be remembered and appreciated."
> Official, Border Services Agency

to consider another perspective. Remember that a departmental official or politician can become your internal advocate if you are willing to understand their constraints and help provide them with what they need to overcome them.

During the opening minutes of the meeting, it is also important not to end every sentence with "but." If an M.P. helped you get access to an official or minister, don't start out by saying, "Well, it was great that you got us in to see the minister, but we feel that a meeting with the prime minister will be more useful. Can you arrange that?"

There will be plenty of time later on to go into the specific problems you are trying to address and your proposed solutions. At the outset your focus should be on establishing a good working relationship based on mutual respect. Above all, avoid giving the impression that no matter what they do, it will never be enough. If the person has fought hard and achieved only a small measure of progress, receiving a long list of further tasks upfront can kill any motivation for more action. Instead, begin the meeting on a positive note by saying that progress has been noted and appreciated. Acknowledging areas where you can find common ground will set a positive tone for the rest of the conversation.

STEP 2: State Your Objectives

As discussed in Chapter 3, outline your SMART objective, framed in a way that links it to the agenda of the government.[4] Emphasize the common things that you and the government are trying to achieve.

Second, be sure to clearly state your specific objective for this particular meeting and how it relates to your broader advocacy goal. It is fundamental to have a clear "ask" for the meeting at hand. Remember that your specific "ask" for the meeting should be something that is well within the power of the individual official you are meeting with. "Improve human rights in Africa" is not going to be effective unless you break it down into specific tasks that can be done by that particular person. If you are meeting with an official the ask could be "Can you raise the possibility of leading a UN Human Rights Commission resolution on the recent violations in Sudan at the next deputy minister's meeting? Can you evaluate my proposal for the reintegration of ex-child soldiers? Can the embassy offer our staff some assistance in reaching remote camps of internally displaced persons? If you are meeting with a minister, can he or she raise the issue at cabinet? A bilateral meeting with the Sudanese? Are there specific questions that demand answers from a department?"

If you are meeting with an M.P., give them questions to ask in Question Period or raise during a standing committee hearing. Ask them to make a statement in the House or engage in advocacy activities related to the issue. Invite the member to participate in

---

[4] Recall that SMART objectives are those that are specific, measurable, achievable, realistic, and time-bound.

community activities, public awareness campaigns, or media events. If they like your cause, the member will want to be identified with it and get on record. Refer back to what politicians can and cannot do for a more detailed list of reasonable requests.

STEP 3: Identify the Problem

How you describe the problem is extremely important. Make sure that you give a concise and relevant brief that is directly related to the issue at hand. Remember that this is your opportunity to give officials a different point of view and you do not want to waste time going over irrelevant information. The best way to do this is to use analytical as opposed to descriptive language to highlight not just what the problem is but also why there is a problem. Try to focus on areas that provide the department with new information.

For example, instead of "Your current program to promote hand-washing among restaurant employees is having no effect. Some owners are following the guidelines and others are not. The money is being wasted and customers are no better off," try, "Your current program to promote hand-washing among restaurant employees is not working because you are targeting the wrong people. Instead of targeting restaurant owners, you should be targeting employees themselves. Our experience shows that when you work directly with the people whose behaviour you want to affect, you get better results."

It is also important to be strategic about how you use your time to give background details. Departmental officials will find it most useful if you offer a specific, constructive critique of the current policy. Don't use the entire meeting to analyze the issue rather than to propose a solution. Focusing on process can be legitimate if your ultimate goal is a fair process itself. When process is not your major objective, however, too much focus on the problem can take attention away from finding a solution. Finally, include why you are making this particular request and a brief description of what you have done to further your cause so far.

> "Avoid 'paralysis by analysis'. Groups can argue endlessly over process and never get to the proposed solutions."
>
> Robin Tourangeau, Former Policy Adviser, Prime Minister's Office

If you are meeting with a minister, this is your opportunity to give an *alternative* brief. From your research, you should be able to anticipate how the minister was briefed in advance. He or she will have the issue framed from the department's point of view. During the meeting, you can brief the minister the way you would like the information to be presented. You can reframe policy questions from an alternative perspective and present information that the minister is not likely to hear from others.[5]

This is also your chance to point out where the department has left gaps, dismissed important information, or overlooked another point of view that should be emphasized. Your added value is that you can outline where *outside* concerns are, rather than concerns within the government.

---

[5] See Chapter 8, "How Do You Get Your Message Out?"

A note of caution. Although you are presenting an alternative brief in your own language, be sure that the basic content of your message is consistent with the message you presented to officials. Remember that both sides communicate and it is important to avoid confusion.

STEP 4: Pose Pertinent Questions to Current Thinking

If you are meeting with a politician, one of your main goals is to give them the tools they need to question the information they have on your issue. A good way to do this is to point out glaring examples of mistakes that can or will occur if the government takes its expected course of action. This will often stick in the member's head to be raised whenever the issue comes up. If the example is really clear, ministers will want answers to these questions from the department before any decision is made.

There was a good example of this we used often while I was at the Department of Citizenship and Immigration. A major policy objective of the department is to prevent people with criminal records from entering Canada. The question the politician cannot ignore is "What about Nelson Mandela? With his history as a political prisoner during the apartheid era, he would be denied." No politician wants to be responsible for an embarrassing incident where a respected world leader is treated as criminal by the government. This one example opens the door for a whole series of deeper, more involved policy discussions: "Clearly, to prevent this problem, the government needs to allow for an exception to the rule for political prisoners. Let's talk about what that might look like."

STEP 5: Present a Credible Alternative

Once you have presented the problem in detail, outline a game plan on what needs to be done. Present briefly the common challenges you are both facing to move the issue forward. Be sure to explicitly recognize any obstacles you know the government is facing in meeting your common objectives.

Refer to Chapter 12 on developing workable alternatives. Here you want to give a detailed presentation of the solution you propose. Be sure to back up your recommendations with an explanation of why you have credibility on the issue. Discuss any specific steps the government can take to address the issue in a positive way. Also be clear about what you are currently doing to address the problem. Tactfully offer yourself as a resource, not just to advocate, but to help work out feasible solutions to unforeseen problems as they arise. Not only will this keep you abreast of all developments on your issue, but it will help build trust and good working relationships as you go along. When presenting your alternative, be sure to include a communications angle. Explain why this can be a good story for the government to tell and offer public support should these steps be taken.

When meeting with a politician, it is important not to leave a feeling of hopelessness. Ineffective meetings are those that just lament insurmountable

> "If you enter the discussion asking for the impossible, you may cut yourself off from a whole range of options that are not only possible, but probable."
> Official, Department of Foreign Affairs and International Trade

problems without proposing possible solutions. Expecting the minister or M.P. to come up with an answer on the spot is bound to be both ineffective and frustrating. They will be looking to you for answers during the meeting.

For politicians, do not go into as much detail as you would with officials but have detailed information on hand to offer if requested. Politicians will not be able to evaluate those details themselves. Rather, the goal here is to get political support for asking officials to seriously develop another option. Ideally, the minister would instruct the department to take your proposal seriously and work with you on developing it. You want to leave a lasting impression that there are other ways to do things that work, and these deserve serious consideration. It is also important to offer something in the meeting, as well as just asking for help. Even if your offer is just to sit down and work out the details together, making the offer sends the message to the minister that you are reasonable and not unduly confrontational.

STEP 6: Listen to Contrary Arguments

How you use your time during the meeting is critical. While you want to cover all your key points, you also want to leave lots of time for others to speak. Officials and politicians will be prepared for their meeting with you and it will be important to hear what they have to say. Expect that there is a lot to learn about why the government is taking its current course of

"A common mistake that groups make is that they fail to thoroughly consider the consequences of the actions they propose. Members want to see that your recommendations are thought through and well researched."
Bill Casey, M.P., Cumberland-Colchester-Musquodoboit Valley

action and what is preventing it from taking another. Also listen carefully for any clues as to where the bottlenecks to moving your proposal forward may be. Once you understand the sources of the official's hesitation, use this information to develop well-researched responses. Make note of any future work you may need to do to address any gaps in your proposal that officials identify.

STEP 7: Outline the Constituency of Support

> "Don't play both sides of an issue. If you do, you will quickly get that reputation among M.P.s. Working with more than one party is entirely legitimate but it is important to be open about it and make sure that the information you provide is consistent."
>
> Honourable Carolyn Bennett, M.P., St. Paul's, Toronto, Former Minister of State for Public Health

For political meetings only, describe who else is with you. Arguments have much more force if there is a coalition of groups that share a particular point of view. It is especially powerful if you have groups from very different backgrounds supportive of your cause. If you can present the member with a list of supporters that includes, for example, an environmental group, an economic think-tank, a police force, and a lawyers' group, that gives them a strong tool to work with internally.[6]

It is very important to be upfront about who else you have met with. If you are associated with one party (e.g., unions and the NDP, church groups and the former Alliance), come clean about why you are meeting with this particular member. Groups with the most success have credibility on the issue itself, rather than through affiliation with one particular party.

---

[6] How to build effective coalitions is discussed in more detail in Chapter 2.

STEP 8: Acknowledge Opposing Points of View and Provide Responses

In meetings with politicians, it is especially important to address other points of view. Politicians will usually. have an immediate idea of where opposition is likely to come from. If you are meeting with the member, you can be sure that others with an opposing point of view are trying to as well.

Meeting criticism head on – by anticipating concerns and giving answers to opposing arguments in advance – is a great way to arm the politician for the inevitable fight to follow. Offer responses that are quick to grasp and easy to remember so that when the member confronts the question, your work can be top of mind. Acknowledging opposing points of view also demonstrates that you have a good grasp of your issue and have taken into account the opinions of others.

STEP 9: Ask Questions to Gather Relevant Information

This is your opportunity to ask the specific questions you had noted during your research phase. The questions should be directed at helping you take the next step. Why do the provinces object? Why are other departments uncomfortable with this? When will the final decision be made? Who will ultimately make the decision? Officials will often be quite open about the difficulties they are facing, and this is a good chance to gather important information about what is going on within the government. Listen carefully to the answers. If you want help to push an issue

> "What are the one to three points I should walk away with? Emphasize your main message."
> Paul Genest, Former Senior Policy Adviser to Prime Minister Jean Chrétien

internally, you will have to help that official overcome the obstacles they are facing if you can.

STEP 10: Restate the Specific Objective for the Meeting and Leave Behind a One-Page Brief

Bring the discussion back to the specific task you are trying to achieve with this particular meeting. Meetings can often go off on tangents and lose the focus on their specific objective. It is usually a good idea to reiterate the specific ask for the meeting to make sure the discussion remains on track.

For politicians, remember that the objective must be relevant at this particular time. Reiterate why this is a good thing for the country, the province, or the community, and why now is the time to act. Be specific about what the minister or M.P. can do to help and explain why those practical steps are important.

A quick "cheat sheet" that includes responses to the most common criticisms is particularly helpful for politicians. If you are meeting with an adviser, leave behind your one-page brief but offer to give the staffer useful supplemental information that the minister may want to have on hand. Any supplemental information should be well organized for quick reference so that the adviser can call it up at a critical time.

With officials, you can leave as much supplemental material as necessary to strengthen your case. Be careful, however, that you do not dilute the main message of your one-page brief by giving a large pile of documents if you are not sure they will be read.

> "Offer yourself as a quick source of information should an adviser need it. Political staff usually have several organizations on speed-dial for someone to call when they need immediate answers at critical moments."
> Former Political Adviser to the Minister of Human Resources and Social Development Canada

At the End of the Day

The more specific your objective for the meeting, the easier it will be to request follow-up. In closing the meeting, ask for a clear response to your question verbally or in writing by an agreed-upon date. Make sure you have the specific name of the person to follow up with. If that date comes and goes with no response, you have a clear reason to call or e-mail to see if your issue was raised as requested. During the follow-up call, ask for any other information you can gather at that time.

After a meeting, call people back to thank them or send thank-you notes to express appreciation. A lot of work goes into preparing these meetings on both sides, and it is important to acknowledge the effort to keep the dialogue going. If you have followed these steps, however, that dialogue will be easier. You will have demonstrated your value to those in government and made a contribution that they can work with. One good meeting can open many doors. When you make a great impression, backed up by useful information and sound credentials, you open up a whole new range of possibilities. After a good meeting, don't be surprised if the government is soon reaching out to you for advice.

> "Send a follow-up letter that is widely copied. The letter should reiterate any commitments made by all sides."
> Alex Neve, Secretary General, Amnesty International, Canada

CHAPTER ELEVEN

WHY DO ISSUES GET STUCK?

Overcoming Obstacles

There is nothing more frustrating than feeling that your issue is up against a brick wall. No matter how hard you push, it just seems as though it will never budge. Hitting an obstacle that seems insurmountable can suck your time and energy and cause you to become demoralized or even want to give up on your cause.

So why do issues get stuck? While some of the reasons for resistance in government may be given as an excuse to avoid change, there are other very tangible constraints that every government official faces when evaluating new ideas. It could be that it's redundant (it duplicates an existing program or is too similar to a program that tried and failed before), too expensive, not well researched, too risky, or just antithetical to the current government's political beliefs and agenda.

There are good reasons that getting a proposal through the system is not easy. Democracy is often about finding the lowest common denominator between opposing points of view. For a decision to be sustainable, it must have some degree of consensus on all sides. When a decision is made without a basic level of agreement – between political rivals, politicians, and the bureaucracy, or different departments within the bureaucracy itself – it is likely to be reversed later on or never implemented properly in the first place.

To understand why your issue might be stuck, you have to ask the right questions that will reveal the obstacles your issue faces. This chapter looks at some of the most common reasons why issues get stuck. It is divided into separate sections that look at obstacles resulting from issues of jurisdiction, timing, and internal and external opposition. The end of the chapter offers suggestions for dealing with these obstacles as they arise.

> "Conflict is the nature of democracy. Don't get frustrated. It will be difficult but don't walk away."
> Jack Layton, Leader of the New Democratic Party

THE WRONG JURISDICTION

One of the most common concerns advocates have is that bureaucrats can indefinitely pass the buck on an issue. A group is told to speak with person X, who refers them to person Y, who tells them to talk to Z, who passes them off to person X all over again. Inevitably, this problem is the result of a failure to find the right jurisdiction.

When governments speak of jurisdiction, they are referring to the right and power to interpret and apply the law. When different levels of government have arguments over jurisdictional issues, they are arguing over the extent of authority or control that a particular decision-maker has over an issue or territory. In some cases, a government may be fighting for more power over an issue because they want to have a greater say about how a policy should be handled. In others, a government may want less responsibility because they do not want to be stuck with the bill.

Often a meeting with the federal government will seem ineffective because your issue is stuck in a jurisdictional loop. This means that the hands of the person you are meeting with are tied because they know that they need the consent of either another level of government or another branch of government to do what you are asking and that these other parties will have major concerns with the proposal for their own reasons. Fights over jurisdiction can be endlessly frustrating for advocates on the outside trying to figure out who is in charge and who has the power to make a change.

A local community in rural Newfoundland, for example, may be pushing their local member of the House of Assembly, Newfoundland's provincial parliament, to prevent development of a certain area of forest by declaring it a national park. He may be supportive of the issue and agree to look into it by talking to officials, or even the minister of the Department of Natural Resources in the Government of Newfoundland and Labrador. This is where the delay will begin. Officials in the provincial department will be hesitant because they know that it is ultimately the Parks Canada Agency of the federal government that has the authority by law to create a national park. The process to do this could involve negotiating a formal memorandum of understanding between the federal and provincial governments and conducting a feasibility study of the area to determine whether status as a national park is warranted. Subsequent meetings with the local MHA, therefore, can seem very unproductive. He may be able to get the ball rolling, but he neither he nor the government he represents has jurisdiction to act on the issue.

Shared Jurisdiction

For some issues, it may be difficult to find out which level of government has clear responsibility. Often this is because your issue is one of shared jurisdiction. Some issues, like immigration, for example, involve complex power-sharing relationships between the various levels of government. In the case of immigration, the Immigration and Refugee Protection Act (IRPA) states that the federal government has a commitment to consult with the provinces when setting immigration levels and the distribution of immigrants across Canada. Although the federal government is generally responsible for the selection of immigrants, there are special arrangements called provincial nominee agreements that set out circumstances in which provinces can select individual candidates according to their own priorities. In addition, there are working groups set up that include federal, provincial, territorial, and municipal representatives to examine a host of issues that cross jurisdictional lines, such as access to professions and trades, business immigration, and language training.

At other times, an issue may be stuck because neither level of government wants to claim responsibility. In one case we dealt with at Foreign Affairs, an international human rights tribunal ruled that Canada was in violation of the principle of non-discrimination because it allowed provincial money to fund private Catholic schools without also funding Jewish and other religious schools. The Conservative provincial government in Ontario (under Mike Harris at the time) had refused to look directly at the issue of funding other religious schools and referred the issue to the federal government. The citizen who launched the case then argued that it is a federal responsibility to make sure that Canada fulfils its obligations under international human rights law. His position was that if the provinces refuse to abide, it is up to the federal government to step in and fund the other religious schools directly. He asked, if Canada ignored the ruling, how could we then say that other countries, with poorer human rights records than our own, should comply with international law?

In this case, concerns over jurisdiction made action difficult, if not impossible, because it brought in a constitutional issue. First, funding for French Catholic schools is an issue that was part of the fundamental agreement between the English and French during Confederation to protect French language and culture. Second, education in general is widely held to as an area under the exclusive jurisdiction of the provinces. Politically, there was little chance that the federal government would now want to claim jurisdiction. To correct the problem and apply a policy of non-discrimination today, the federal government would almost certainly trigger a constitutional debate. This would mean opening up not just the one constitutional issue, but *all* the constitutional issues we have struggled with for years. After the failure of Meech Lake, it was clear that the federal government would be unlikely to risk a constitutional debate over this one particular case. Therefore, the federal government's response was that education is a provincial responsibility. Officials essentially said, "If you don't like your provincial government's response, wait and elect a new one." Consequently, for years the plaintiff was repeatedly passed back and forth between the provincial and federal governments, with neither one agreeing to claim jurisdiction.

Although the relationship may be complex, what is important to know from an advocacy perspective is that shared jurisdiction on your issue will mean your strategy may have to address several levels of government at once.

Common Points of Contention between Levels of Government

To understand the underlying dynamic going on in these intergovernmental discussions, it is important to be aware of some persistent causes for tension.

The federal government transfers large sums of money to the provinces and territories to take care of various social programs. The main transfer programs are the Canada Health Transfer and the Canada Social Transfer, which are used to fund health care, education, and social assistance programs; equalization payments, which go to the less prosperous provinces so they can provide comparable public services without raising taxes; and the Territorial Formula Financing, which goes to the territories to address the additional costs of living in Canada's remote north.

Because the federal government is transferring so much money, federal departments often want to attach strings to the programs or have some oversight on how this money is spent. The provincial governments have the opposite point of view. Because they are responsible for the delivery of the most important social programs in the country, they feel that they know best how the money should be allocated. As a result, provincial governments are often pushing to have fewer strings attached so they can spend the money with more autonomy.

While municipal governments deal with more local community issues such as snow removal and fire protection, they remain under the jurisdiction of the province. The key difference at the municipal level is that you are mainly dealing with individuals, as opposed to members of a caucus that can act as a team. Second, although these individuals are more dependent on the bureaucracy for information, the bureaucracy is not as sophisticated as the public service at the provincial and federal levels. Provincial governments are much larger, in their resources and personnel, than municipal governments. The result is that the information the politicians are getting at the municipal level tends to be less detailed. At city council, there is also no political staff to offer independent advice. It is a much more direct relationship between citizens and their representatives, who have a more independent role in decision-making.

Jurisdiction Within and Between Government Departments

Aside from jurisdictional issues between levels of government, there are also jurisdictional issues or "turf wars" within and between government departments themselves. Other departments working at the same level of government may want to or have to be consulted on a given issue. As departments compete with each other for resources within the budget cycle, they may be competing to control certain issues that demand a greater share of overall government resources and attention.

If the official who reviews your brief knows that other governments or other departments will have problems with it, they will likely send you to those officials first to see if you can resolve the problems in advance. Officials at all levels know that they cannot take a proposal forward without some level of consensus from other levels of government that share jurisdiction. If your proposal offers a new approach that involves some risk, many officials will not want to step up and assume that risk if they know they will be wandering into an intergovernmental mess.

Clearly it is important to make sure that you are dealing with the appropriate jurisdiction. This means you are talking to the right person, at the right level of government, in the right department at the right level of the hierarchy.

In general, the federal government in Ottawa is responsible for issues that concern the whole country, as one nation. This would include questions of national defence, international trade, the environment, border security, immigration and refugee policies, federal taxation, agriculture, foreign aid, and foreign affairs.

At the federal level, it is the job of the Intergovernmental Affairs Department (which is located within the Privy Council Office) to monitor all potential sources of conflict with other levels of government and work on possible solutions. Other federal departments, such as Industry Canada, have designated bureaus (the International and Intergovernmental Affairs Branch) that are responsible for managing complex intergovernmental jurisdictional issues on their department's behalf.

Provincial governments in Canada are generally responsible for education, the delivery of health care, property and civil rights law, licensing, prisons and law enforcement, and the general administration of justice in the province. Each province's Web site has a link to a general list of ministries and organizations.

When it comes to municipal issues, it is important to know that all provincial governments have explicit constitutional jurisdiction for municipalities. In other words, municipalities are framed by provincial laws and in some cases (i.e., Quebec) do not have any direct relationship with the federal government. As such, control over issues at the municipal level is usually a discussion of whether the province or the municipal council will pay the bill.

THE WRONG TIMING

The timing of a decision is almost always political. Although this book recommends that every advocacy strategy work both top-down (at the political level) and bottom-up (at the bureaucratic level), when it comes to the timing of a decision, political factors are the most important consideration. Chapter 6 focused on when to advocate for your cause, and this section will look at some strategies for when timing becomes a major obstacle to moving your issue forward.

At times, it can be very difficult to determine when a particular decision will be made because of the main challenge in any government office – volume. For ministers in particular, every day is a struggle to balance competing priorities and manage the daily paper flow. This will include memos requesting a specific action, approval of a trip, draft cabinet presentations, draft legislation, memos on international meetings, and all official correspondence. All memos that reach a minister for decision are usually on a tight deadline, meaning that the decision needs to be made by the end of that day or soon after. Your proposal may be stalled because it just isn't at the top of the right person's agenda due to the urgency of other issues competing for their time on a given day.

If your issue is not chosen as a priority it doesn't mean it can't become one. If an issue generally handled by the department is brought to the minister's attention, he or she does have the power to override almost any departmental matter. The challenge for the minister is to choose priorities – which issues to get involved in and follow closely.

Elections

Elections are a good time for public awareness work, but a terrible time for policy advocacy. Smart politicians simply do not make promises that they are not sure they can keep. As a candidate, they do not have access to departmental resources to thoroughly analyze a policy and know what can work. They also don't know if they will become a minister and what the new cabinet's specific priorities will be once elected. Candidates can, however, promise to devote attention to the issue and make it a priority if elected.

This is where public awareness work can be very useful. Campaigns to raise awareness of an issue and push all parties to take it on as a priority can be very successful. If your cause becomes an election issue, you will find all parties clamouring to differentiate themselves and push the issue as far as possible.

If you are a member of a particular party, you can also try to influence the policy platform by becoming

> "Politicians will sometimes be looking for the 'big idea' to run on. If your issue meshes with the agenda of a particular candidate – bring it to their attention."
> Campaign Manager, Nova Scotia Provincial Election, 2006

a delegate to the party convention and voting on potential priorities. Be aware that although the party as a whole may adopt an issue and make promises to move it forward, the party platform is used as a basis to guide cabinet decisions but does not become policy directly. For example, the Liberal party platform of 2006 promised to amend the Constitution to remove the federal government's ability to overrule the Supreme Court. If elected, there was no guarantee that they would be successful in complicated constitutional negotiations. The party platform sets a goal only, by which citizens can measure the party's success.

INTERNAL OPPOSITION

In Chapter 4 we discussed how divisions both within and between departments can influence a policy decision. In this section we'll look at intra- and inter-departmental consultations more closely because failure to address internal opposition to a policy proposal can become the main obstacle to taking your issue forward.

Intra-Departmental Opposition

At the early stages of policy development, the lead bureau in a department must get approval on an initiative both horizontally, from other bureaus in the department, and vertically, from officials higher up in the hierarchy.

Let's look at a policy proposal within Foreign Affairs as an example. An officer in the Latin America and Caribbean Bureau puts forward a proposal to increase the time and attention paid by the Government of Canada to Haiti because assisting Haiti will strengthen Canada's reputation in Latin America as a whole. The proposal includes a request to increase the number of ministerial visits, phone calls, and letters to Haiti as well as to increase Canada's profile in helping to build important infrastructure. First, within the bureau, the officer must get agreement on the specifics of the proposal and draft a memo outlining the new policy direction. This will need to be signed off by the director general, who will determine whether Haiti is a priority for the Latin American and Caribbean Bureau as a whole. Once the DG has approved, the memo will likely be sent up to the assistant deputy minister of bilateral relations.

The memo will be raised at some form of intradepartmental consultation. There, other bureaus will ask a number of questions. Will this take time or resources away from our priorities? Will the work be carried out in a manner that is consistent with our objectives? For instance, the Youth Internship Program may have spent a year getting a departmentwide commitment to seeing a greater portion of department funds going to youth-related projects. They will want to know whether the plans for Haiti place a priority on youth. Other bureaus may also ask, have we tried this in the past? What worked? What didn't? What did we learn from our experience? If the proposal inhibits other bureaus from pursuing their goals, officials may attempt to kill the proposal before it gets off the ground. Ultimately, it will be up to the deputy minister to balance the various concerns and decide whether the proposal becomes a priority for the department. If the issue also touches on the work of other departments in the government, the deputy minister or assistant deputy minister may insist that the proposal be discussed at inter-departmental consultations.

Inter-Departmental Opposition

Government departments are designed to act as checks and balances on one another and have a legitimate role to play in questioning a given course of action initiated by other departments.

Going back to our Haitian example, if Foreign Affairs wins internal consent to take the proposal to inter-departmental consultations, it will take a unified position and present the proposal as a departmental priority. Other departments will then be given the chance to ask questions from their own perspective or raise objections. They will look at questions such as these: Will Foreign Affairs cover the entire cost or will it cost us as well? Will this set a precedent that will be difficult to uphold? Will this lead to other countries expecting a similar increase in resources? Will this infringe upon our jurisdiction or goals?

If the Canadian International Development Agency has decided to place its priority on Africa that year, for instance, they may be concerned about the Government of Canada sending mixed messages. CIDA may raise an objection, arguing that increasing time and attention to Haiti will lead to a "slippery

"If a department loses an interdepartmental battle, it is often because there are real consequences that had not been considered. These can include a loss of jobs or a weakening of safety standards. More often than not, the concerns raised by other departments are not frivolous. If officials raise good points during the meeting it is better to acknowledge that you hadn't considered something and would like to take another look. Remaining adamant when there are clear problems with a proposal will only affect your credibility in a negative way."

Official, Treasury Board

slope" of other countries demanding a similar increase in resources.

Other departments will also want to know whether the proposal is likely to have any impact on their daily operations. The Border Security Agency will want to know whether there will be any new cause for increased attention to security concerns. The Justice Department will want to evaluate whether there will be any legal implications. There may be ongoing court cases that could be affected if another part of the government proceeds with a seemingly unrelated policy position.

While getting a proposal through all consultations can seem like a formidable task, for the most part, lead departments are capable of working out many of these kinks along the way, before the proposal gets to the political and parliamentary level.

When a major concern is raised between departments, the lead department may try to address the problem several ways. First, they may try to allay concerns by pointing out that the benefits of proceeding outweigh the costs. Second, they may try to get as many allies onside as possible, so that the source of opposition is isolated in trying to block the proposal. Third, departments may send the proposal up to the political level for elected officials to make a political decision to proceed. The minister of the lead department can make political arguments to other ministers, who can ask that the nervous departments back off. Finally, most of the time, the lead department will take suggestions from other departments or bureaus and incorporate them into a slightly modified position. When this is done, departments can head off problems in advance, before they get to the political level.

Political Opposition

Once the proposal has been widely consulted on, a memo will go up to the lead minister for approval before it goes to cabinet. The memo will include a description of the positions of other departments and what efforts were made to address concerns. If some of the concerns were unable to be resolved, the memo will give the minister a heads-up that an opposing department will likely brief their minister to raise an objection to the proposal in cabinet. In evaluating whether to approve the memo, the minister's office will then consider whether this is a good decision for the minister politically. Should he or she put their reputation on the line for this proposal? What outside groups are pushing for or against the decision? What sort of political precedent will this set? Will the minister be able to justify it when faced with the demands from other communities? Why the Haitian community and not the Sri Lankan one?

Before making a final decision, the lead minister's office will usually check with the ministers of any opposing departments to see where their thoughts are. Will they agree with the remaining concerns of their department and argue against the proposal at cabinet? Can they convince the minister that, politically, this is the best course of action for the government as a whole?

EXTERNAL OPPOSITION

To be successful, it is important to figure out who else is active on your issue outside of government and what their position is. To get started, here is a list of potential places opposition can come from.

Opposition Parties

In a majority government, the opposition parties rarely have the power to stop an issue from proceeding or push an issue through the House, but in a minority government they can have a much more direct impact on government policy. In a majority government, the opposition is mainly concerned with holding the government accountable through Question Period, debates in the House, and their work on parliamentary committees. Opportunities such as official Opposition Days become very important as they allow minority parties to criticize the government or draw attention to an issue the government would rather ignore.[1] In this context it can be useful to work with opposition parties to raise awareness of your issue and put pressure on the government to act. Choosing to work with the opposition, however, can be politically risky – for you and/or your organization. It is a matter of timing. If your work with government departments and ministers is going well, you may want to hold off on increasing pressure from the outside until you run out of other options. By going to

---

[1] There is approximately one Opposition Day per week, or twenty per year, while Parliament is in session.

the opposition while ministers and departments are still working with you, you can lose your access to those on the inside who are actually drafting the details of the policy.

The major difference in a minority situation is that there is less power in the executive branch of government (the prime minister and the ministers of the cabinet) and more power in the legislative branch (Parliament). This means that in a minority government, opposition parties can join forces to block important government objectives or hinder progress on key government initiatives. In the spring of 2006, for example, three opposition parties joined forces in the House of Commons to pass a motion that embarrassed the government for failing to present a concrete plan for Canada to meet its environmental targets as part of the Kyoto Protocol.

Minority governments also present real opportunities for opposition parties to have a direct influence on government policy. In order to get legislation passed, the governing party may have to make specific concessions to garner enough votes. If your advocacy campaign is at a standstill with the party in power, you can work with one or more of the opposition parties to block initiatives you are not in favour of or push for changes you would like to see. In 2005, for example, the Liberal government of Paul Martin was able to pass the budget only by making concessions to the NDP. Similarly, legislation to legalize same-sex marriage required support from both the NDP and the Bloc Québécois. The ultimate power of a minority government is the threat of a non-confidence motion to defeat the government. If a non-confidence motion passes, the Constitution requires that the government resign or dissolve Parliament and call a general election.

Other Civil Society Groups

On most issues, there will inevitably be other civil society groups both for and against your cause. These may include environmental lobbies, churches, special interest organizations, or professional groups such as the Canadian Bar or the Canadian Medical associations. Local community groups or ethnic organizations may also have a high stake in speaking out on your cause. Remember that the biggest danger coming from other civil society groups is the possibility of "divide and conquer." If groups that would seemingly be your allies on the issue are contradicting or opposing you, politicians will be unwilling to take sides and will often opt for the safer option of the status quo.

Of course, few groups have the time to survey the full range of civil society organizations for their position on an issue. It is possible, however, to identify the major groups that are likely to have a high profile and take a vocal stance. A visit to these organizations' Web sites will often give you a sense of whether they are planning to play a major role in your particular area of concern. Once you do identify a major organization that is likely to be against your issue, find out why. Where does their research come from? Do they have credibility? What messages are they going to put out and is there a way you can counteract them?

Independent Experts

Likewise, independent experts can be either allies or opponents. If the expert happens to support your cause, you're in luck, and they can be a very strong ally in an advocacy campaign. If, however, they have a different point of view, they can also pose a major obstacle to having your message heard.

If there are experts in favour of your cause, find out how you can help them make your case. If they are against your issue, see if they have a rival in their field. Only a person with the same level of credibility will be able to counteract expert research with a divergent professional opinion.

SUGGESTIONS FOR OVERCOMING COMMON OBSTACLES

For all the obstacles mentioned above, the best strategy is to learn where the sources of opposition are coming from and present a stronger case. Decision-makers will want to hear opposing arguments and your response to them because ultimately, once the decision is made, they will face the same kind of questioning from the public.

But what if you've done all the homework, had the meetings, and still feel as though you are getting nowhere? Here are some practical options to help you meet common challenges as they arise.

Option 1: Change the Decision-Maker

"Changing the decision-maker" seems like an impossible task for someone working on the outside of government, but it is actually something that happens often. The easiest way to do this is to appeal directly to those higher up. Once something becomes a direct issue at a higher level, it is unlikely to be delegated back downward. This is especially true for issues that are brought to the attention of ministers or their political staff. If a minister or a deputy minister knows that an issue is likely to generate some public controversy, their office will want to monitor the issue and likely play a role in the final decision.

When Should You Use This Option?

The option of changing the decision-maker can be useful if you are dealing with a decision that has been delegated to a lower-level official and your efforts at that level are getting nowhere. Before you go higher up, however, make sure you do the research so that you don't jump too high. It is usually best to go up the hierarchy slowly, one level at a time, rather than jump immediately to the top. Changing the decision-maker can also be useful when you observe a clear bureaucratic/political divide. If you know that the bureaucracy is dead set against an idea but politicians are likely to be in favour of it, it can make sense to put the issue into the political realm.

> "When they are passing the buck – go higher. Jump up a level and point out the problem. Go the staffer, minister, or committee chair and point out that there is a problem and it needs to be fixed. Make sure you choose a person who actually has the authority to say, okay, let's find a solution."
>
> Political Adviser to a Former Minister of Natural Resources

How Can You Mitigate the Risks?

Going over someone's head will not make you friends. If this is an official you will need to work with in the future be sure to weigh the importance of the current issue against the possibility of being cut out of future discussions. It is important to use the option of changing the decision-maker wisely to preserve your credibility and capital. You don't want to be labelled as someone who will run to a boss at every opportunity. If you do decide to go over an official's head, let the person know you will be speaking to their boss and why. At times, it can even make sense to ask the official for their advice on how to best approach those at a higher level. If it is an issue that an official has been pushing for internally, they may even view your intervention as a helpful way to let their bosses see the reaction to a policy first-hand.

Also remember that appealing straight to the top too early is almost always a mistake. If you go directly to the prime minister or even a minister, their office will want to know whether you have helped lay the groundwork of support that is needed to implement a new policy proposal. Remember that all high levels need to depend on the lower levels to make a change happen. Politicians may be willing to go against their officials, but they will always be mindful of preserving good relationships wherever possible.

Option 2: Force the Timing of a Decision

Of course it is by no means possible to control the timing of most government decisions. You can, however, take an educated guess at when a decision is likely to be made. Drawing upon the discussion in Chapter 6 on good timing, you can ask yourself or those you are meeting with some fundamental questions to decipher what the current priorities are and how your issue may or may not fit into them. Are there major upcoming international meetings that the department or minister is likely to be involved in? Is your department or minister preoccupied with introducing new legislation or testifying before a committee on a specific bill? What are the demands of the parliamentary schedule? Is the government collectively focused on trying to get a major initiative passed? Is there a domestic event, such as a party convention, that may be the number one priority? When are major programs up for renewal? Certain programs are known to be renewed every five years.

State visits, international trips, public forums, high-profile conferences, and commemorative days are all hooks that can link your issue with the government's agenda. Tying your cause to specific events that are the focus of the government's attention is an excellent way to bring your issue to the top of the agenda. If you do discover that your cause is just not a priority, however, there are ways to try to make it one.

For large organizations with international appeal, one way to force the timing of a decision is to offer a private invitation to a high-profile visitor. Nelson Mandela, the Dalai Lama, and Bono are all examples of individuals who were invited to Canada privately, by one or more civil society groups. Once a visit is confirmed, issues that were not seen as a priority for the government often become one.

You can also affect the timing or profile of an issue by organizing a large-scale event. Conferences, annual general meetings of large organizations, concerts, and festivals are all ways to garner attention from the government. The civil society groups active on HIV/AIDS, for example, worked hard to have Toronto chosen as the site for the 2006 World Conference. Once it was on the agenda, the government was under intense public and media pressure to make a series of decisions within a certain time frame to be ready for Canada's announcement. When it failed to do so, the government's lack of action raised the profile of the issue in the public's eye and damaged the credibility of the Conservative Party with regard to HIV/AIDS policy.

Another way to force the timing of a decision is to take a look at a minister's schedule for upcoming trips. Ministers' offices are usually very open about planned trips and the media often report on them in advance. If a minister is booked to go to Africa, for instance, raising an issue related to Sudan can force the issue into the limelight. As discussed in Chapter 8, a good strategy here is to try to get the media to focus on your issue as one of the key questions for the trip. Once the media are onto it, the minister and government will know that an answer must be prepared.

Option 3: Build Larger Coalitions, Bridge Differences
One of the most direct methods of increasing pressure on any level of government to act is to build a larger

coalition, which may involve bridging your differences with potential allies. When a diverse coalition
of organizations is united, it is very difficult for the
government to ignore that common position.

The way to build such alliances most effectively
is to look at your issue from several different angles
before you put forward a proposal. Try to anticipate
where internal and external criticism will come from
and why. The more you can address the concerns of
others in advance, the less likely it is that those concerns will become a major obstacle to moving your
cause forward.

It is also important to try to get as much broad
political support as you can. Find out if a caucus committee is active on your cause by going to home Web
sites of the political parties. Usually the committees
have a general theme such as "Economic Prosperity"
or "Social Justice," so it is possible to tie your specific
issue to an area they are interested in. Do some
research to find out whether the committee as a whole
or individual members of the committee have taken a
position on your cause in the past and what that position was. If at all possible, try to involve members of
the committee in your public awareness activities and
campaigns. Write to the chair of the committee and
offer to make a presentation on the issue at a special
session of caucus. Most importantly, be aware of what
they are doing and when they are doing it to see if
there is any tie-in to your issue.

How Can You Do This?

One of the best ways to demonstrate that there is broad support for an issue is to work on coordinating joint letters between a number of advocacy organizations. Although ministers do not have time to read every letter directly, a staff member is sure to bring a joint letter from several major organizations to the minister's direct attention. Joint letters are even more powerful when they come from a diverse group of supporters who have a common concern about an issue. Once again, these joint letters will have the most impact if the objectives are framed strategically and the timing is good. Following up with a meeting with the minister – where representatives of all participating organizations are present – will reinforce the message that there is concern about the issue across several sectors. This will put even more pressure on the government to make sure it has as substantive a response as possible.

It is also a good idea to see if you can build a more diverse coalition by finding allies in unexpected places. If you can link your cause to a specific aspect of the broader government agenda, it may allow you to consolidate allies who are not at the front line on your topic. For example, advocates for women's groups found that they were getting nowhere in their efforts to raise attention to the issue of violence against women. Instead of continuing to focus on access points for women's issues only (such as women's caucus or specific bureaus of departments with a mandate to address women), they decided to change strategies and link their issue to the government's broader agenda on public safety. Suddenly they found they had allies in non-traditional places. They found common ground with law enforcement agencies and officials concerned with national security. The result was a strong and diverse coalition pushing for an issue that could be included in the government's agenda.

Joint meetings and press conferences can also be a powerful way to garner attention from the government. Used wisely, they can help create a groundswell of support that the government will need to respond to. This option does require a note of caution, however. When a group or individual tends to run to the press after every meeting or small setback, they can become discredited and shut out of internal discussions. If used too often or not effectively, press conferences can backfire by shutting you out of further discussions instead of getting a place for you at the inner table.

Option 4: Isolate the Problem and Work on Other Aspects of the Issue

Fortunately, most issues have several facets. Isolating where the obstacle is and working on another part of the problem will help you make efficient use of your time. If you find that one specific objective is running into an obstacle that seems insurmountable, switch your focus to another aspect of the problem. At times, working out the details in another area can help ease the resistance or open up new ideas for how to approach the original problem.

If you are feeling unsatisfied with the progress on your issue to date, it may be time to take a step back and look at your efforts with an objective eye. Where are you getting blocked? Is this something that just takes a convincing argument or are there complex government constraints involved? Are the jurisdictional issues too complex to resolve anytime soon? Is the proposal just way over budget? On the other hand, are there some areas where you have seen movement? Why is that the case?

If you are finding that the reaction to your proposal is consistently lukewarm, do more research on the benefits of going with the initiative exactly as you proposed it. Try to isolate exactly where other people's objections are and see if you can present other options.

Option 5: Wait for a More Conducive Environment

This is perhaps the most difficult decision of all. This book has tried to simplify how government functions. In practice, policy processes are not all ideal. There are individual personalities, ideologies, and ambitions involved. At times, these can present obstacles that are illogical and very difficult to overcome. It is important to realize when an issue is just not going to move because a constraint is too large to overcome. Don't waste six months on an issue that is not going to go anywhere. Waiting does not have to mean giving up. Over time, the political environment can drastically change. When you have clearly hit obstacles that are extremely difficult to overcome, making the decision to wait for a more conducive environment will only help you by preserving your motivation and making the best use of your current time and resources.

CHAPTER TWELVE

WHAT DO YOU SUGGEST?

Working on Solutions

The best advice I ever received in government came from my chief of staff, who had worked as the second in command to two cabinet ministers after spending several years in the office of the prime minister. This advice can be summed up as "Bring solutions, not problems."

Perhaps the biggest challenge facing decision-makers today is the sheer volume of material confronting them. Whether you are speaking with a minister, M.P., or bureaucrat, if you just outline a list of problems for them to solve you are unlikely to get any kind of satisfying response. As we have seen, ministers and M.P.s do not have the time and resources to think through each issue and develop the solutions themselves. They have to rely on the expertise of government departments to analyze the options and present them with feasible solutions. In doing so, of course, departments present ministers with the solutions they believe are best. Like any large organization, departments can be preoccupied with increasing their resources and expanding their turf. With today's volume, ministers can direct and control only a small portion of a department's activities, leaving officials with a great deal of autonomy to use their power as they see fit.

Advocates who ask government for all the solutions are in for a long wait. If your topic happens to be one that is already a priority for the government, a good solution may be forthcoming. Nine times out of ten, that solution will represent a compromise between various points of view and will not be fully satisfying to any one party. If your topic is not even on the government agenda, waiting for government-led solutions will be even more frustrating.

> "A great question to ask officials is 'What do you need from us?'"
> Official, Industry Canada

The government needs help to shape the best possible solutions to our collective problems. Government departments can only go so far; it is up to citizens who feel the direct impact of government policies and live with their consequences every day to help with the painstaking process of going through the details and figuring out what works.

The key is to help develop solutions that are workable from the government's point of view. Once again, this does not mean compromising on your values. In fact, it means aggressively pursuing concrete progress to create the society you would like to see.

To do this, you have to enter the fight early, when

ideas are not yet set in stone.[1] Recall all policy proposals must ultimately undergo a thorough departmental analysis to make sure that they are feasible from the government's point of view. If that analysis is cut short or bypassed, the result is usually that the policy will never be implemented properly. If you want to shape that analysis, it is therefore necessary to get in there early and offer plausible solutions while a policy is still being developed.

Along the way, however, it is critical not to ask for the impossible. Asking for the impossible usually amounts to no more than an exercise in frustration both for the people you are appealing to and for yourself. When the opening line of a meeting is "Cut off all relations with China," everyone on all sides of the table knows that the meeting is not going to get very far.

Now that we have outlined some of the most common constraints of government, we are in a good position to shape policy objectives so that they offer a realistic alternative to the status quo. Developing a plausible option for the government to consider is essential to seeing your proposal taken up and put into practice.

> "Don't go in with a bottom line that sets the bar impossibly high."
> Official, Treasury Board

Why Worry about Bureaucratic Problems?

One of the most disturbing trends in Parliament over recent years has been the tendency for more and more legislation to be "framework" only. Framework

---

[1] This point is discussed in more detail in Chapter 7, "Which Method Is Best."

legislation, as it is called, is legislation that contains only the general principles that guide major policies. The "details" of how those policies will work are increasingly left to regulation. Although all legislation has to go through the House of Commons and Senate for approval by elected officials, government regulations do not have to go through the same level of public scrutiny. Government regulations can be changed simply by a department publishing the intended change in what's called a "Regulatory Impact Analysis Statement," or RIAS. Once a RIAS is issued, the public is given a minimum of thirty days to comment. After thirty days, a department is free to consider whether it will heed the advice received during that time. There is no obligation to alter the regulations based on comments received from the public. Although the lead minister can be approached by groups who want to register a complaint about a regulatory issue, more often than not regulations are considered too detailed for the minister or the minister's office to get involved in directly.

The advantage of framework legislation is that it gives the government flexibility to respond to frequent changes more easily. The Immigration and Refugee Protection Act of 2002 is a good example. The law states that immigrants may be granted landing if they meet "the selection standards established by the regulations."[2] The regulations contain a detailed points

---

[2] The Immigration and Refugee Protection Act, 2002, p. 80 Section 6. (1).

grid that sets out different categories that influence selection, such as education, language, or "adaptability." The regulations also denote what the overall passing or failing score is to be admitted into Canada.

Placing this information in regulations gives the government flexibility to alter the emphasis between all the factors (education, language, ties to Canada) as changes in the economy require. It also allows the government to change the ultimate pass mark, which has an immediate effect on the number of immigrants in the queue who will meet the necessary criteria.

But what are the consequences of this flexibility? Essentially, government officials can drastically alter who gets into Canada without a full review by Parliament.

The more disturbing aspect is that in the transition to framework legislation, some rights-based questions are being delegated to regulations. This means that government departments have more power to alter or modify questions that affect fundamental rights, without full parliamentary oversight and public participation. Of course, it is not feasible to have Parliament involved in the details of every government policy. But too much framework legislation can narrow the space for open, democratic debate.

The most practical implication of this for those interested in having an impact on government policy is that the role of officials is increasingly important. As we have seen, departments play a powerful role in determining what options are laid out before ministers. Because so many important policies are being left to regulations to be implemented, officials also have a critical role in making decisions that are not scrutinized by the public eye. For this reason, advocates must develop a detailed understanding of bureaucratic concerns so that they can help formulate options that withstand bureaucratic constraints. If you can come up with solutions that take into account governmental constraints, your proposal will have a better chance of being taken up as government policy. The following offers a step-by-step guide to help you develop and present them.

> "Start with the assumption that the government wants to hear you, and they don't yet understand your perspective."
>
> Official, Border Services Agency

HOW TO DEVELOP WORKABLE POLICY ALTERNATIVES

STEP 1: Identify a Common Policy Goal

Begin with a shared purpose that both you and the government are trying to achieve. If you both have in mind a common goal, take for granted that the government's objective is to try to achieve that goal in the best possible way. At the outset, if you can offer your experience as a credible source of information, the question then becomes how to spend the taxpayer's money to achieve the best results.

A good example comes from the Halifax Initiative's 2006 policy brief on Export Development Canada (EDC) and Human Rights.[3] The Halifax Initiative is a coalition of development, environment, faith-based, human rights, and labour groups that in

---

[3] The full brief can be found on their Web site at www.halifax-initiative.org/updir/PolicyBrief-EDCandHR.pdf.

2006 participated in a series of government round-table meetings on the extractive industries and corporate social responsibility. Export Development Canada is a federal Crown corporation set up to support and develop the capacity for Canadian companies to engage in export trade and respond to international business opportunities. It is therefore the main source of publicly supported export financing in Canada. The brief opens by emphasizing a shared goal, as stated in EDC's own business code of ethics: "To promote the protection of internationally recognized human rights."

STEP 2: Offer a Specific, Constructive Critique of the Existing Policy

It is important to make sure that your critique of existing policy is accurate and specific. Avoid broad sweeping negative comments that are too general to be helpful. It is also a good idea to include a few points that catch attention, could easily be turned into a headline, and therefore are difficult to ignore politically.

Going back to the Halifax Initiative's brief, they begin their critique as follows:

> Projects that EDC has funded – such as the Urrà dam in Colombia and Three Gorges dam in China, the PT Tel Pulp and Paper Mill in Indonesia, and the Antamina Copper mine in Peru – have had serious human rights impacts. These include arbitrary arrest, use of paramilitary "security" forces, forced resettlement, poor labour conditions and impacts on worker health,

disappearances and kidnappings, inadequate consultation and compensation, environmental destruction, loss of livelihood and destruction of sacred and spiritual sites.

Once you've pointed out the problem, demonstrate that you have researched and analyzed what the government (or, in this case, Crown corporation) is already doing to try to address it. Focus on describing why the current approach is inadequate.

EDC did not sign a memorandum of understanding with the Department of Foreign Affairs (DFAIT) to strengthen internal communications and the exchange of information on human rights. It now uses classified information from DFAIT, as well as other public material to get an overview of a country's human rights situation. This feeds into a larger assessment the crown corporation conducts to identify potential and political market risks (to EDC and its clients) of conducting business in a specific country. In theory, human rights issues may increase the risk rating beyond a threshold that is too risky for EDC, but there is no predetermined level of risk that effectively vetoes a project.

STEP 3: Explore Options

Before attempting to "reinvent the wheel," explore whether there are options presented by other individuals, organizations, or government institutions. Do you agree that they offer a credible alternative to the status quo? Can you combine resources to offer a more substantial analysis of possible solutions?[4] More often than not, large organizations are happy to help put you in contact with others working on a common goal. Similarly, your local M.P. or provincial member's office may be able to help you identify who else is working on the issue and how you may reach them to assist in building a stronger or more thorough case.

In the example of the Halifax Initiative, the brief discusses how successful models for human rights screening do exist. They describe a number of credible mechanisms that are currently being used by other institutions and companies.

> The Norwegian Agency for Development has developed a human rights screening mechanism for development projects, and the UN High Commission for Human Rights is developing a human rights impact assessment for trade policies.

STEP 4: Analyze Your Proposal from the Perspective of Government Constraints

Using the guide from Chapter 11, evaluate your proposal from the perspective of basic government constraints. Anticipate where opposition to your proposal is likely to come from so that you can address possible concerns in advance.

"Make your argument from different perspectives and think of new angles to strengthen your case. A social argument, an economic fact, and an international comparison present a convincing case."
Katharine Cornfield,
Citizenship and
Immigration Canada

---

4 Refer to Chapter 1 for more information on connecting with others working on your issue.

A. *Jurisdiction* – Are you dealing with the right people, in the right department or institution, at the right level of the hierarchy? Make it a priority to find out what constraints the officials you are working with are facing so that you can help to overcome them.

B. *Timing* – Why is this issue not a priority? What is the department or institution currently preoccupied with?

In this case, the brief points out that "the Danish Institute for Human Rights has even designed a tool for companies that corresponds to the structure of the business unit and only takes 40 hours to implement."

> "Come in prepared to compromise and recognizing that you are not going to get your whole way."
>
> The Right Honourable Joe Clark, Former Prime Minister of Canada

C. *Internal Opposition* – Do you anticipate that other departments will have objections to your proposal? What about other divisions within the lead department? Do you anticipate political support or opposition to your idea? From which politicians?

D. *External Opposition* – Are there any other outside groups that may oppose your recommendations? Are there independent experts advocating a different point of view? Are there caucus groups or opposition parties that may take issue with your proposal?

Although all these factors may not apply to your issue, it is a good idea to simply try to put yourself in the other person's shoes. The more you understand where they are coming from, the more you can tailor your recommended solutions so that they have the best chance of being adopted.

STEP 5: Present Your Solution

Above all make sure that any proposal you offer can be backed up by reliable and credible sources. If you are seen as a legitimate source of additional research and information, an alternative perspective can be very useful for officials developing the options to be presented for decision. It is particularly useful if you can point to successful precedents.

Going back to our example, the Halifax Initiative's final proposal is that EDC "should develop a human rights impact assessment mechanism for screening the impacts of projects on human rights, based on existing models." This recommendation is a good one because it is specific, measurable, achievable, and realistic.[5]

As you share your ideas with others, it is important to listen well to the feedback you are getting and respond. If unanticipated constraints to taking your proposal further are pointed out to you, acknowledge them and plan to do more work. This is a good way to show that you are not blindly adamant about your issue just for the sake of taking a strong position. It is also a good idea to demonstrate that you are a reasonable partner to work with by offering to help find answers when good questions are raised.

Finally, it can also be a good idea to present options for consideration. These may include phasing in a particular policy or testing it out in a controlled

> "Explain why this is a good story for government to tell."
> Paul Genest, Former Senior Policy Adviser to Prime Minister Jean Chrétien

---

[5] For more on good recommendations, see Chapter 3 on defining clear objectives.

environment. If you begin negotiations with one absolute position, it will reduce your chances of being able to address problems as they arise. By contrast, presenting options with room to manoeuvre will help build your credibility and increase your chances of success.

CONCLUSION

Ten years ago I was working for a student activist organization in San Francisco. I'll never forget the day I met Kevin Danaher, a hero of the anti-globalization movement and author/editor of numerous books.[1] Sitting in a semi-circle, I was part of a group of students listening to Danaher as he eloquently laid out a devastating case against the world's most powerful international financial institutions. ". . . to the World Bank, development means growth. But single-mindedly pursuing growth is the basic ideology of the cancer cell. . . ."

---

[1] Including *50 Years Is Enough: The Case Against the World Bank and the International Monetary Fund* and *Corporations Are Gonna Get Your Mama: Globalization and the Downsizing of the American Dream.*

I remember feeling surprised, and as the discussion went on, restless. Kevin had an uncanny ability to plant a firm sense of injustice deep in your gut.

> "... The policies imposed by the World Bank and the International Monetary Fund are designed to ease the repayment of debt. Money that could have been invested in health, education and housing has instead been transferred to wealthy bankers. . . ."[2]

I found myself craving solutions. I was hoping that he would finally give me the magic answer, a clear action that would lead to immediate results. But when it came, I remember feeling that something wasn't quite right.

He said, "The World Bank and the IMF need to be abolished."

This is where he lost me. Did he mean wiped out completely? Wasn't the World Bank the institution with a budget of billions of dollars and a mission to fight poverty and improve the living standards of people in the developing world? Wasn't the IMF a mechanism to help bail countries out of financial crises and avoid the economic conditions that led to the depression of the 1930s? How would wiping out these institutions solve these problems? If we did manage to dismantle them, what would we replace

---

[2] Danaher's comments are further explored in his book, *50 Years Is Enough* (South End Press, 1994).

them with? Would the new institutions be any better?

I remember shyly raising my hand.

"Why don't we just flood the bank with good people and design better policies?" I asked.

I'll never forget Kevin's response. He made a noise like a giant *sploosh* and pretended to throw a bucket of ice cold water on me. He said, "Come on, kid, wake up! Are you dreaming? Nothing short of revolution is going to fix these institutions. They're rotten from the inside out and need to be destroyed and rebuilt anew."

I was embarrassed, but I also felt that if I adopted his point of view, it would lead to an extremely frustrating career. I had visions of myself twenty years later, cynical, disillusioned, and still feeling as if all my efforts had led to no results. I knew that it was not the route I wanted to take.

I can understand why people choose a radical approach. There are times when an analysis of a problem leads to a fundamental flaw in the system itself, one that needs to be addressed at its source. Those who are looking at creating alternative institutions hold out hope that the answers to our persistent problems of poverty, insecurity, and environmental degradation lie in forming new institutions altogether.[3]

---

[3] There are now plans to create a new regional "Bank of the South" as an alternative to traditional multilateral financing options like the World Bank. The governments of Venezuela and Argentina have both pledged more than $1 billion to get the idea started, with several other countries across Latin America and parts of Asia expressing interest in participating. Critics of the World Bank hope that the Banco del Sur will be free of institutional flaws like having voting privileges based on financial contribution.

Clearly, there is a role for non-violent radicals, like Danaher, to push for new systemic approaches to solving our most complex problems. And I am not recommending that reform replace the radical approach to social change. However, from what I have seen from the outside and the inside of government, there are too many radicals and far too few reformers. Turning up at a G8 protest is just very late. We need more citizens willing to connect to the political system and use the democratic mechanisms we have available to seek change from within.

Members of Parliament need your help. They need your help to keep them informed of the issues that are having an impact on your community. Ministers need your help to ask the right questions of their bureaucracies and make sure that they have full information before making a decision. And officials need your help to make sure that the policies they are developing are relevant and useful to those they intend to benefit.

Of course, Parliament remains our central institution to hold the government accountable to its people. But the more people disassociate themselves from the politicians they elect, the more we undercut their ability to truly represent our views. Moreover, beyond Parliament, democratic governments are facing the unavoidable reality that they must also maintain a continuous dialogue with their citizens. The big issues of our day – climate change, endemic poverty, the spread of disease, and threats to our security – are so complex that states must draw upon every resource available to them.

Informed networks of citizens add valuable experience, analysis, and expertise to the search for global solutions. In Canada, we have seen what can be accomplished when government and citizens' groups focus on a common goal: the Ottawa Convention that bans antipersonnel landmines, the creation of the International Criminal Court, and the campaigns against sexual exploitation and the military enlistment of children are just a few examples of what can happen when the energies of government and citizens' groups are combined.

Having an impact is possible. Whatever your level of experience and resources, the main conclusion that I hope you'll come to from reading this book is that in Canada, it is possible to become an effective voice on an issue that you care about. Stop thinking about *if* and start thinking about *how*.

FOR FURTHER READING

BOOKS AND ARTICLES

Saul D. Alinsky, *Rules for Radicals: A Pragmatic Primer for Realistic Radicals* (Vintage Books, 1971).

Robert Barnard, Dave Cosgrave, and Jennifer Welsh, *Chips and Pop: Decoding the Nexus Generation* (Malcolm Lester Books, 1998).

John Bejermi, *How Parliament Works* (Borealis Press, 1976).

Kim Bobo, Steve Max, and Jackie Kendall, *Organize for Social Change: Midwest Academy Manual for Activists*, Third Edition (Seven Locks Press, 2001).

David Bornstein, *How to Change the World: Social Entrepreneurs and the Power of New Ideas* (Oxford University Press, 2004).

André Carrol, *Citizen's Hall: Making Local Democracy Work* (Between the Lines, 2001).

C.E.S. Franks, *The Parliament of Canada* (University of Toronto Press, 1987).

Joseph Heath and Andrew Potter, *The Rebel Sell* (HarperCollins Publishers Ltd., 2004).

Michael Ignatieff, *Human Rights as Politics and Idolatry* (Princeton University Press, 2001).

Michael Ignatieff, *The Lesser Evil: Political Ethics in an Age of Terror* (Penguin Canada, 2004).

George Lakoff, *Don't Think of an Elephant: Know Your Values and Frame the Debate* (Chelsea Green Publishing, 2004).

George Lakoff, *Moral Politics: How Liberals and Conservatives Think*, Second Edition (University of Chicago Press, 2002).

Robert MacGregor Dawson and William Foster Dawson, *Democratic Government in Canada* (University of Toronto Press, 1989).

Patrick Malcolmson and Richard Morley Myers, *The Canadian Regime: An Introduction to Parliamentary Government in Canada* (Broadview Press, 2005).

Elizabeth May, *How to Change the World in Your Spare Time* (Key Porter Books, 2006).

Joseph Nye, *Soft Power: The Means to Success in World Politics* (Public Affairs, 2004).

Jededian Purdy, "After Apathy," *The American Prospect* 11, no. 2 (December 6, 1999).

WEB SITES

Online resources on policy advocacy and communications:
www.amnesty.ca

www.ccic.ca

www.cic.ca/whoswho

www.charityvillage.com/cv/ires/ires1.asp

www.imaginecanada.ca

www.spinproject.org

www.thepraxisproject.org

Online media links:
www.canajun/com/canada/current/media.htm

www.cna-acj.ca/client/cna/cna.nsf/web/online

www.cs/cmu.edu/Unofficial/Canadiana/
CA-zines.html

www.synapse.net/radio/print.htm

Key government Web sites:
www.canada.gc.ca

www.canada.gc.ca/othergov/prov_e.html

www.direct.srv.gc.ca/cgi-bin/direct500/BE

www.parl.gc.ca

ACKNOWLEDGEMENTS

My sincere thanks to the International Development Research Council and the Canadian Council for International Cooperation for supporting this project from its inception. I would like to specifically thank Sue Cass, Brian Tomlinson, Michael Stevens, Sara Kemp, and Kristen Ostling for their insight, experience, and good advice. Thanks to the Bogliasco Foundation for the opportunity to bring the idea to fruition.

My deepest appreciation goes to Samantha Haywood, Elizabeth Kribs, and Chris Bucci for supporting this project from the beginning and helping to shape it all the way through. Thanks to my mentors, Elinor Caplan and Dan Costello, who continue to guide me in all my pursuits. I am grateful to Natalie Brender, Rob Cohen, Debra Felsted, and Andrew Morrow who offered ongoing support and encouragement. A final thank-you to Robin Neinstein whose creative contribution to any project is invaluable. And, of course, thank you Brian for the million and one things you did every day to make this project a reality.

Josh Randell

Amanda Sussman is currently Policy Adviser to Plan Canada, one of the world's largest international child-centred development organizations without religious, political, or governmental affiliations. *The Art of the Possible* is Sussman's first book. She lives in Toronto.